RELEASED

INSPIRATION FROM THE FIRST LOCAL CHURCH VENTURE INTO WORLDWIDE MISSIONS

THE ACTS 13-14 JOURNEY

STEVE BURCHETT

*Released: Inspiration from the First Local
Church Venture into Worldwide Missions*

Copyright © 2022 by Steve Burchett

This first edition published by Christian Communicators Worldwide.

CHRISTIAN COMMUNICATORS WORLDWIDE
P.O. Box 12045
Parkville, MO 64152

Cover and interior design by Tony Barmann.
All rights reserved.

Purchase additional copies of this book at www.ccwtoday.org.
For information about this and other
publications write info@ccwtoday.org.

Scripture taken from ESV® Bible (THE HOLY BIBLE, ENGLISH STANDARD VERSION®), copyright © 2001 by Crossway, a publishing ministry of Good News Publishers. Used by permission. All rights reserved.

ISBN 978-0-9820968-5-7

ALL RIGHTS RESERVED
No part of this publication may be reproduced, stored in a retrieval system, or transmitted in any form by any means — electronic, mechanical, photocopy, recording, or otherwise — except for brief quotations in printed reviews, without the prior permission of the publisher. Subject to USA copyright law.

Contents

How to Use Bristol Series Books 5

Introduction 7

Map: First Missionary Journey 12

Chapter 1: Everybody 13

Chapter 2: Sender 23

Chapter 3: Priority 35

Chapter 4: Message 45

Chapter 5: Message (continued) 53

Chapter 6: Response 63

Chapter 7: Tenacity 75

Chapter 8: Reach 87

Chapter 9: Aim 99

Chapter 10: Aim (continued) 109

Chapter 11: Participants 119

Chapter 12: Now 129

Acts 13-14: Full Text 137

How to Use Bristol Series Books

The Bristol Series is for thinking Christians who desire to study single passages in a deeper way, complete with background information and careful attention to the context and details of the passage.

Here are recommendations when studying with others:

For weekly group study, we suggest reading the chapters of the book aloud together rather than at home individually between meetings. You may wish to collect the books and redistribute them each time you meet until the class is completed. You might read aloud each week a larger portion of the Biblical text (in the back of the book) before reading the smaller portion and the chapter for that session. This will orient the group if any were missing, and will deepen understanding and discussion.

The first lesson should include reading the Introduction, the full Bible text at the end of the book, and chapter 1. That's slightly more reading than the following weeks, but is necessary to have the initial background. The remaining chapters will include reading the smaller portion of Scripture before the chapter, and the chapter itself. You may ask the participants to occasionally read the entire biblical text at home, further enhancing the study. Discussion questions follow each chapter. Please add your own questions as time allows.

Introduction

My first international trip for ministry was memorable before I even arrived at the final destination. I was headed to Manila, but the flight from Japan to the Philippines took an unexpected turn, and then another, and then another. At first, we felt the typical turbulence. Then, ever-so-calmly, the pilot announced that we would be taking a different route than normal because *we were going around a typhoon*!

Soon the bumps turned into dips, always accompanied by multiple "Ahhhs!" of passengers. At one point, the shakes and thuds became so severe that strangers started to grab on to one another. The lady next to me suddenly gripped my arm and *would not let go*. Even when the winds calmed down, she was trying to hold on. I pulled away and tried hard to keep space between us. She probably wondered why I got up and went to the restroom so often.

Finally, Manila.

Yet the adventure was not over. The woman would not leave my side. I had to figure out how to get away from her. And then it happened: there among the jumbled up crowd of Filipinos, I saw a sliver of light. With my carry-ons in-tow, I took off for the thin opening, running like I was trying to catch my next flight! I never saw the lady again.

I went on to have a wonderful experience in the Philippines. The ministry included speaking at a jam-packed church leaders' conference (200 men were expected, far more than that came), preaching in multiple settings (including a prison), and meeting with various missionaries and ministry workers in order to encourage and learn from them. What a first international ministry experience!

Since that trip, I have traveled multiple places throughout the world for ministry, such as Ethiopia, Uganda, Romania, and India. I have enjoyed a coffee ceremony in Addis Ababa, and a boat ride on the Indian Ocean. More importantly, I am now an eyewitness to God's growing kingdom in all of these locations. I have gathered with Ugandan believers for a church meeting under a mango tree outside of Kampala. Multiple times through the years in Gohatsion, Ethiopia, I have taught pastors and church planters who traveled many hours by foot through rugged terrain, before enduring several hours more by bus to arrive at the teaching location. And a couple of hours outside of Mumbai, I have taught classes of future church planters and leaders, listening to sometimes eleven or twelve different languages being spoken as the students vigorously worked together in small groups, interpreting Scripture.

Sadly, I have also seen poor examples of both visiting and indigenous missionaries and pastors in most places I have traveled. Some are not effective leaders because they have had very little training, or unhelpful teaching and unhealthy church experiences in the past. I am always eager to open Scripture with men like that if they are willing to listen to the Lord. But there are some who are lazy, or greedy, or proud, and maybe all of the above. This is a lamentable reality.

Why mention all of this? I do not think ministry experiences around the globe are necessary in order to understand

Acts 13-14, the passage under consideration in this book. However, I hope my exploits will be an aid when we think about how these chapters speak to the church today. My trips have not only given me unique insights about what is happening on the ground, but they have caused me to ask, "Is what I saw right? Is this what the head of the church wants?" With an open Bible, I have thought long and hard about those questions. Part of that study has involved "traveling" countless hours with Paul and Barnabas on their first journey. I am so glad you are about to take that trip with me.

A couple of tips will improve your study. First, a map is provided before chapter 1. Follow the entire journey on this map, even paying attention to the miles covered. This will be interesting to consider because it concerns a time when there were no automobiles or airplanes. Tracing the journey will be a visual reminder that you are reading a historical record of what happened in the first century on that soil, among those mountains, along those bodies of water, and on those roads and paths. To aid your use of the map, each chapter (except the first and last) begins with information regarding the "Starting location" and "Cities on the journey" for that particular section.

Second, the entire text of Acts 13-14 is included in the back of this book. I hope you will read it right away, and perhaps multiple times throughout the weeks of study. Also, be sure to read the smaller portions of Acts 13-14 that precede each chapter of this book. Take seriously what I wrote, but the Bible must always be the priority.

Here is a sobering thought from J.C. Ryle: "The moment we open the Bible the devil sits down by our side." Therefore, before you do anything else with the study of Acts 13-14, and each time you delve into these chapters, do not forget to pray!

Steve Burchett
Parkville, Missouri, USA

CCW's Bristol Series is for thinking Christians. We aim to provide readable, exegetically careful, and background-rich treatments of single texts of Scripture designed to speak strongly to critical issues in the life of believers. They are accompanied by discussion questions for study groups and mentoring.

Christian Communicators Worldwide, www.ccwtoday.org

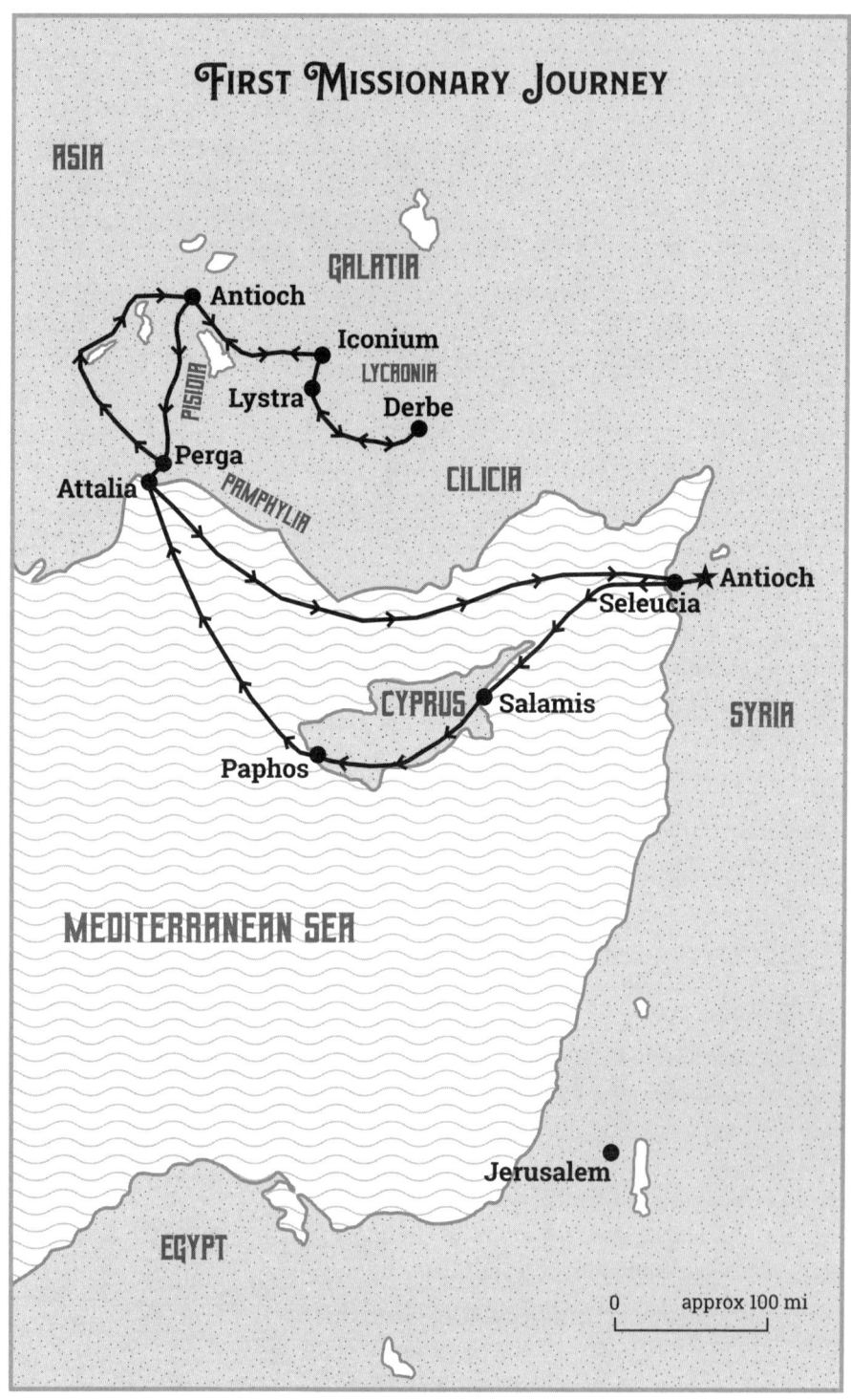

Chapter One

Everybody

There is something about the topic of missions that causes some believers to say, "Nope, not for me." And since Acts 13-14 is typically titled, "The First Missionary Journey," you might think the content is mostly for missionaries. My aim in this chapter is to prove otherwise.

The Gospel

Centrality

In Acts 15:36, Paul was reflecting back to the first missionary journey when he urged Barnabas, "Let us return and visit the brothers in every city where we proclaimed the word of the Lord, and see how they are." So the main activity of these men on the first journey was this: "in every city" they "proclaimed the word of the Lord."

Multiple times throughout Acts 13-14, the gospel message is highlighted either by a summary statement or through evangelistic encounters. I will not list them all here, but stay alert when reading these chapters and you will quickly see how vital the message about Christ was.

Some leaders in our day downplay the importance of doctrine. Paul and Barnabas, however, believed that doctrine — specifically "the word of the Lord" (13:44) or "the gospel" (14:7) — was essential. It does not get any more "doctrinal" than the gospel! The content of their message was so important that after they returned from this journey, they were eventually dispatched to Jerusalem for the "Jerusalem Council" to insist that salvation is by grace alone through faith in Jesus Christ (Acts 15:1-21).

Acts 13-14 reminds missionaries of the objective content that must be at the center of their ministries. However, *every* believer needs to hear again and often that there is only one message that will save that spouse, that coworker, that neighbor, that relative, that child.

Power

These chapters also portray the gospel's power to save lives. For example, early in the journey, Sergius Paulus "believed" (13:12). In Pisidian Antioch, "many Jews and devout converts to Judaism followed Paul and Barnabas, who, as they spoke with them, urged them to continue in the grace of God" (v. 43). And then other Gentiles believed (v. 48). In Iconium, "a great number of both Jews and Greeks believed" (14:1). In Derbe, the gospel was proclaimed producing "many disciples" (v. 21). That is power!

The gospel continues to change lives today. A young lady was converted to Christ out of a background of deadly drugs, online prostitution, and relations with witches, spiritists, and other evil people in the context of pagan religions. By her own confession, she should have died multiple times. But through online videos and the only Christian she knew, she heard the gospel and was saved! Here are her own words about being set free.

December 9th was the day of my salvation: my surrender. Before meeting with my brother in Christ, I remember thoughts of the enemy festering in my mind to cancel the meeting, but God was stronger and I met with him. We talked, prayed, and cried. The day lasted about nine hours. My friend walked me through the gospel and I surrendered to Christ that night. He gave me his Bible and instructed me to read through the Gospels immediately and pray constantly.

After praying and surrendering to the Lord that night, I got a trash bag and ripped all the tapestries off my wall, all my new age pictures, dream catchers, crystals, tarot cards, books, idols, and more: I threw it all away. Trashed it. I did not care what my family was going to say. My grandma that night said to me, "You can't just change like that." I looked up toward the sky and said, "This is the truth. Yes I can." Because it was all the Lord. He opened my eyes. He gifted me the gift of faith, repentance, and supernaturally caused me to be born again.[1]

The gospel is "the power of God for salvation" (Romans 1:16). That is just as true sitting on your child's bed as when a missionary shares the good news in a mud hut in Africa.

Missions and the Local Church

How did this powerful gospel spread?

Consider the bigger picture in Acts. Before his ascension, Jesus said to his apostles, "But you will receive power when the Holy Spirit has come upon you, and you will be my witnesses in Jerusalem and in all Judea and Samaria, and to the end of the earth" (Acts 1:8). Then, in Acts 2, he poured

---

[1] "A Gospel Testimony," https://www.reformandamin.org/articles1/2020/5/20/a-gospel-testimony, accessed May 23, 2020.

out the Holy Spirit upon his people. The rest of Acts shows the gospel going forward through Spirit-empowered followers of Jesus, first in Jerusalem (chapters 2-7), then in Judea and Samaria (chapters 8-12), and finally "to the end of the earth" (chapters 13-28).

The Holy Spirit's early implementation of the Abrahamic blessing (i.e., salvation to the world through Abraham's seed, Jesus; cf. Genesis 12:1-3; 13:15; Galatians 3:16) in Acts 1-12 led to extensive evangelism, starting in Jerusalem. God worked in multiple ways to eventually get the gospel "to the end of the earth." For example, immediately after the pouring out of the Holy Spirit at Pentecost (Acts 2), spontaneous apostolic ministry occurred out of the Jerusalem church. Then the persecution of believers in Jerusalem propelled the gospel far beyond that city as "those who were scattered went about preaching the word" (8:4), taking the gospel "as far as Phoenicia and Cyprus and Antioch" (11:19). In Antioch, we meet the first group of believers in a city outside of Jerusalem called a "church" (11:26), though we should assume local churches were also established in other locations where people believed and were baptized (cf. 9:31).

Philip and Peter are two of the men God used to advance the gospel far and wide prior to Acts 13. Philip, because of the persecution in Jerusalem, went to Samaria where he enjoyed fruitful ministry (8:5f). He then led the Ethiopian eunuch to faith in Christ on the road to Gaza (8:26-40). Peter first peached the gospel within Jerusalem, but then went to locations outside of that city, including Caesarea where his ministry to Cornelius (10:1-48) became the subject of a heated debate back in Jerusalem regarding what was necessary for a Gentile to be saved (see 11:1-18).[2]

---

[2] Therefore, as New Testament scholar Eckhard J. Schnabel notes, "The 'mother church' of the Gentile mission was Jerusalem." *Paul the Missionary: Realities, Strategies and Methods* (Downers Grove, IL: InterVarsity Press, 2008), 71, Kindle.

All of the above demonstrates that God's plan to advance the gospel to the nations[3] was well under way *before* Acts 13. But Acts 1-12 does not *specifically* tell of any sending out of missionaries through an organized effort of a local church. What makes Acts 13-14 unique and so instructional for our day is that, for the first time in Acts, details are given about a local church who self-consciously engaged in the setting apart and sending out of missionaries for "the work" (13:2) of worldwide missions. The church then welcomed those missionaries home once the "work" was "fulfilled" (14:26). Though the Jerusalem church had breached the barrier of the Gentile world, a new chapter in world missions began at Antioch.

A question churches should ask is, "How should our church be involved in missions?" Acts 13-14 is an excellent place to begin answering that question. Once again, we see that these chapters are for *everybody*.

Motivation to Persevere

As you read about the spread of the gospel through missionaries who were intentionally sent out of a local church, something else is supposed to happen in your heart: Acts 13-14 is meant to motivate you to keep loving and following Jesus.

Both the Gospel according to Luke and Acts are addressed to "Theophilus." He was presumably a real man in a governmental role because the first time Luke wrote him, he addressed him as "most excellent" (Luke 1:4).[4] Luke and Acts are a two-volume work. In the first volume, Luke wrote to bolster the faith of Theophilus and other believers of that day, and he

---

[3] Throughout this book, I use the term "nations" to refer to people groups (ethnic communities throughout the world; cf. Revelation 5:9), not political states.

[4] See Acts 23:26; 24:3; and 26:25, where Luke addressed the Roman governors Felix and Festus with the title "most excellent."

did this by writing a well-researched, rational, orderly account (Luke 1:4) about "all that Jesus *began* to do and teach" (Acts 1:1, emphasis added). Acts is about what the risen Jesus *continued* to do, by his Spirit, through his people. It tells the story of the next thirty years beyond the resurrection and ascension of Jesus.

During these decades, God directed the advance of the gospel and the building of Christ's church as believers took the gospel "to the end of the earth" (Acts 1:8; cf. Luke 24:27). Just as with his Gospel account, Acts was meant by Luke to be a reassuring, endurance-promoting narrative.

Acts 13-14 fits perfectly into this bigger purpose of Acts. In these chapters Luke showed Theophilus (and other believers like him), likely a Gentile, that the ministry of Jesus continues, and that the people of God includes not only believing Jews, but believing Gentiles throughout the world. It was as if Luke was saying, "And here is the story of the gospel spreading far beyond Jerusalem. Jesus is not only the Savior of Israel, but of the nations! He not only saves Jews by faith alone, but also Gentiles!" Luke was urging the original recipients of Acts not to give up on Jesus.

This story is intimately connected to us as well; it is *our* story. We read in Acts 13-14 about real people who took the gospel to other real sinners. Some heard and believed. These new believers then shared the gospel with their neighbors and their children. Once again, some responded by submitting to Jesus. Some of these believers were eventually sent out to other unreached locations around the world.

Centuries passed until, one day, the gospel arrived in your country, and in your city or in your little community, and the gospel was believed by some. Then somebody told you about Jesus, or somebody gave you a book about the gospel of the kingdom, and you repented and believed. And now you care about others hearing the good news, so you try to tell them about Jesus through your words, or literature, or you invite them to gatherings where they will hear the truth.

If you are a believer, it is because of what happened in Acts 13-14. The Holy Spirit worked through a local church and two men in particular to fire the gospel across Asia and eventually Europe, and then ultimately to every continent, including yours. Empires and other kingdoms have come and gone, but God's kingdom remains and advances. It will continue to do so until King Jesus comes back and gathers all of his people and fully establishes his kingdom on a new earth full of righteousness and peace and joy.

If you are a believer, you will probably one day meet Sergius Paulus in the kingdom, or the people who believed during Paul's ministry in Pisidian Antioch and Iconium and Lystra and Derbe. They are our brothers and sisters. Their Savior is our Savior. This should fill us with gratitude and increase our love for Jesus, and it should encourage us to keep following him, which must include fulfilling our role in getting the good news to the lost around the world, whether we are missionaries or not.

Now that you are convinced (if you were not already) that Acts 13-14 is a significant portion of Scripture for *everybody*, not just missionaries, we are ready to begin our careful study of the text. In the next chapter, we will ask, "Who sends missionaries?" The answer might surprise you.

Questions for Discussion

Before discussing these questions, it is best to have read the Introduction, the text of Acts 13-14 (found in the back), and chapter 1 of this book. Remember, because of important background material, the reading for this chapter will be considerably longer than the others.

1. Looking at the text of Acts 13-14, which "episode" stands out to you? Why?

2. What sections or verses of Acts 13-14 appear to be the most difficult to understand?

3. In chapter 1, what is the most convincing proof that Acts 13-14 is not just for missionaries?

4. What do you anticipate you might learn from studying Acts 13-14?

1 Now there were in the church at Antioch prophets and teachers, Barnabas, Simeon who was called Niger, Lucius of Cyrene, Manaen a lifelong friend of Herod the tetrarch, and Saul. 2 While they were worshiping the Lord and fasting, the Holy Spirit said, "Set apart for me Barnabas and Saul for the work to which I have called them." 3 Then after fasting and praying they laid their hands on them and sent them off.

4 So, being sent out by the Holy Spirit, they went down to Seleucia . . .

Acts 13:1-4a

Chapter Two

Sender

Starting location: **Antioch (in Syria)**

Cities on the journey: **Seleucia (seaport)**

We need to think briefly about the term "missionary." That English word is not found in most versions of the Bible. The earliest use of "missionary," a word derived from Latin (*mitto*, "I send," and *missio*, "mission"), is tied to the Jesuits in the 16th century.[5] The equivalent word in the New Testament is "apostle."

One reason we use "missionary" instead of "apostle" today is because we do not want to promote the idea that men with the authority of the twelve apostles or the apostle Paul, foundational apostles (cf. Ephesians 2:20), are still functioning in the church. This book is not the place to hash out whether or not we should still use the word "apostle" (in a non-foundational sense). Instead, I will stick with the word "missionary" throughout, using it specifically to refer

---

[5] J.D. Payne, "Currents of Change: How Did Everything Become Missions?" in *Mission Frontiers* Vol. 41, No. 6, Nov/Dec 2019, 28.

to messengers of Christ who have been sent to evangelize the lost *and* establish churches. So, whenever I reference missionaries in this book, I will be referencing men[6] who function like Paul and Barnabas did during the first missionary journey (see Acts 14:23; cf. Titus 1:5), not, for example, someone who goes out to evangelize or serve in a hospital or theological institution (as important as those ministries may be).

In keeping with this narrower definition of "missionary," I will also refer to "missionary workers" or "missionary helpers." They serve under the direction of a missionary, similar to John Mark in Acts 13. These workers may be male or female.[7] They assist the missionary and are often worthy of financial support in order to serve on the missionary's team. Some male missionary workers will help the missionary by teaching and appointing elders in his stead. This was the role Titus fulfilled on the island of Crete and Timothy in Ephesus and the surrounding region, both under the apostle Paul's authority.

This matters in a study of Acts 13-14 because these chapters describe two men going out from the church in Antioch to proclaim the gospel and gather believers into local churches. Paul and Barnabas, both called "apostles" in Acts 14:14 (cf. v. 4), model the type of ministry that should characterize missionaries today.

With those clarifications understood, we are ready to go back to approximately A.D. 46 and consider a journey that was the genesis of the message of grace coming to the whole world.

---

[6] Because missionaries exercise authority over men through, among other activities, appointing elders, and will have an extensive teaching ministry, the role of "missionary" should be reserved for only qualified men and not women (see 1 Timothy 2:11-15; Titus 2:1, 15).

[7] For female illustrations of this, see, for example, Priscilla (Romans 16:3), and Euodia and Syntyche (Philippians 4:2-3).

Who sends missionaries?

Who sent out Paul and Barnabas on the first missionary journey? You might quickly respond that it was the church in Antioch. But to be precise, the correct answer is the Holy Spirit: "So, being sent out by the Holy Spirit . . . " (13:4a). However, Acts 13:3 says the church "sent them off," but that does not mean the church was *ultimately* responsible for commissioning and sending out these two. New Testament scholar David G. Peterson explains.

> [T]he verb translated *sent them off (apelysan)* has the sense of 'release', 'dismiss', or 'send away' (e.g., 3:13; 4:21; 5:40; 15:30, 33), not 'appoint.'[8]

Paul and Barnabas were "sent out" by the Spirit and "released" by the church from their present ministry in Antioch to a new realm of service far beyond that city. This somewhat technical detail is significant because it reveals the Lord's heart for the missionary enterprise.

Additionally, Acts 13:2 tells of the Holy Spirit spurring the first missionary journey: "While they were worshiping the Lord and fasting, the Holy Spirit said, 'Set apart for me Barnabas and Saul for the work to which I have called them.'" The Holy Spirit was at least speaking to the five "prophets and teachers" mentioned in verse 1 (the nearest antecedent of "they" in verse 2). Perhaps the Spirit spoke through one of the prophets when he communicated his plans for Barnabas and Saul (i.e., Paul, v. 9).

Missions is the Lord's idea. Over a decade before this commissioning, when Paul was converted, the Lord used a believer from Damascus named Ananias to minister to Paul.

---

[8] *The Acts of the Apostles* (Grand Rapids, MI: Wm. B. Eerdmans Publishing Co., 2009), 377.

Ananias was reluctant because of Paul's wickedness toward Christians in the past (Acts 9:13-14), "But the Lord said to him, 'Go, for he is a chosen instrument of mine to carry my name before the Gentiles and kings and the children of Israel'" (9:15). What occurred in Acts 13 was something that the Lord had planned long ago, and now the Holy Spirit was actively moving Paul (with Barnabas) to his apostolic calling to take the name of Jesus to the nations out of a local church.

What about the church?

Even though the Holy Spirit is the instigator and director of the work of missions, the church is not passive. They not only released the men, but consider how Acts 13 begins: "Now there were in the church at Antioch prophets and teachers, Barnabas, Simeon who was called Niger, Lucius of Cyrene, Manaen a member of the court of Herod the tetrarch, and Saul." The diversity of these men is evident: Barnabas was a Levite from the island of Cyprus (4:36); "Simeon who was called Niger" was a black man (his nickname meant "black") probably from Africa; Lucius was from Cyrene located on the northern coast of Africa; Manaen was a "lifelong friend of Herod the tetrarch," that is, Herod Antipas, who was the king in Galilee during the time of Jesus' ministry (cf. Matthew 14:1; Luke 3:1; 23:8); Saul was a former Pharisee from Tarsus in Cilicia. This was a team of leaders that understood the gospel was for people of all ethnicities and cultures, Jews *and* Gentiles.

The people in the church were also primed to engage in getting the gospel to the world. Antioch, the capital of Syria, was about 300 miles north of Jerusalem (not to be confused with Pisidian Antioch, 13:14f). It was the third largest city in the Roman Empire with possibly 250,000 people, approximately 90% Gentiles.[9] Into this mostly pagan city came persecuted

---
[9] Schnabel, *Paul the Missionary*, 70.

believers from Jerusalem (cf. Acts 8:1b; 11:19). They shared the good news, and because "the hand of the Lord was with them," people were converted and a church began (cf. 11:19-21).

It was such a remarkable occurrence for so many Gentiles in Antioch to believe in Jesus that when the church in Jerusalem heard, they sent Barnabas to confirm it (11:22). Barnabas then traveled about 150 miles to Tarsus and found Paul and brought him back to minister with him in Antioch (11:26). Paul's calling as apostle to the Gentiles, and his probable previous experience ministering to Gentiles, no doubt motivated Barnabas to persuade Paul to join him.

It is not a surprise that out of a church with this composition the Holy Spirit sent men to take the gospel to the nations. The believers in Antioch knew by experience that the gospel was for Jews *and Gentiles*, and Barnabas and Paul were uniquely prepared to go, especially after spending a year teaching in Antioch (11:26b) and serving among such a diverse team of leaders (13:1).

Ready to be Sent

We should not only appreciate the wisdom of the Lord in using the church in Antioch to get the gospel "to the end of the earth," but we should also learn from that church's example. The Antioch church actively cooperated with the Holy Spirit in the work of missions in at least two ways.

First, the church in Antioch had men who were ready to be sent by the Holy Spirit.

The five "prophets and teachers" were "worshiping the Lord and fasting" (vv. 1-2). The word for "worshipping" is probably better translated "serving," indicating that "they" (the five prophets and teachers) were serving by using their gifts, and at the same time they were fasting, expecting the Lord's blessing in some way. They were doing what the Lord wanted them to do, and ready to do whatever else the Lord desired. That is the setting for when the Holy Spirit commanded, "Set apart for me Barnabas and Saul for the work to which I have called them" (v. 2).

What is often not considered when reading Acts is that the book spans about thirty years, even though all twenty-eight chapters can be read in less than three hours. It is easy to read multiple chapters and think it is only covering a few weeks or months, when sometimes it is surveying several years.

In the case of Paul, even though the first account of his conversion is in Acts 9, the events of Acts 13-14 took place over *thirteen years* after his conversion. Those intervening years were full of both ministry and learning so that by the time he was sent out, he was a mature and capable leader. And Barnabas was already a believer and ministering before Paul's conversion (cf. Acts 4:36-37; 9:27), so he also was seasoned and significantly prepared for the ministry ahead. As mentioned above, these men had spent a year together serving in Antioch, and just prior to the Spirit's commissioning in Acts 13, the two men had traveled together to Jerusalem bearing a financial gift for the Jerusalem church in their time of need due to a famine (11:27-30; 12:25). These capable, trustworthy men were the Antioch church's first missionaries.

This does not intimate that only men who have impressive resumés should be sent to the mission field. There are various roles that can be filled on a missionary's team. But when a church is participating with the Holy Spirit in sending out a man to proclaim the gospel and plant churches, he must be a knowledgable, gifted, courageous, self-directed man who is above reproach.

Where do these kinds of men come from? Certain gifted men might come into the life of a church for a season, similar to Paul and Barnabas, and then be released to the mission. However, it will more likely be necessary to develop men in the church. How does this happen?

Experiencing a healthy church

Fundamentally, future missionaries need to experience healthy church life. A "missions-minded" church should see the value of having vibrant body life because this is what the Lord wants to reproduce around the globe. It is difficult to "plant" what you have not first experienced. All believers should feel responsible to give future missionaries the kind of church life that will help them to start gospel-embracing, flourishing churches.

Receiving training by an elder[10]

Elders (pastors) in a church also have a strategic role in developing future missionaries. They can do this by first training all of the men in the church, and then pouring into some more than others with the aim of developing their skills and gifts for ministry. In our church, each elder meets with a group (or groups) of men (covering all of the men) once a week primarily to study passages and books of the Bible and to stimulate application of what is studied. The fruit of this weekly learning is mature men.

Pastors must also give men opportunities to serve, including in the areas of teaching and leading. How else will they be able to discern if a man is gifted in those ways that are required to be a missionary?

---

[10] In the New Testament, "elders," "pastors" (shepherds), and "overseers" refer to the same male leaders in a church (cf. Acts 20:17, 28; Ephesians 4:11).

Serving as an elder first?

Finally, it's possible, and maybe preferable, for a man to first serve as an elder in a church before he departs for the mission field. Shepherding a flock with a team of pastors, which often involves dealing with weighty matters, will equip him for missionary work. And if a man is going to appoint elders (Acts 14:23), it will be advantageous for him to have been an elder previously. Even serving as an assistant to an elder provides remarkable benefits for a future missionary.

We love you!

Second, the church in Antioch released their missionaries in a way that said, "We love you and are with you!"

"Then after fasting and praying they laid their hands on them and sent them off" (Acts 13:3). As in verse 2, is "they" referring to only the three remaining among the prophets and teachers, or the whole church? Even if it is a reference to only the three, they represented the whole church who, when Paul and Barnabas returned, were all present and ready to hear the missionaries' report (14:27).

These co-workers of Paul and Barnabas set aside food once again (cf. v. 2a) to seek the Lord and pray for these brothers, entrusting them to the Lord before they headed into difficult territory. And then they "laid their hands on them" (v. 3) as if to say, "We are with you, we are for you, and we love you."

At some point, we will know that it is God's will to send a man. Having prayed and trained and considered God's providential workings, and after assessing opportunities and evaluating a man's readiness (including his family, if married), a missionary prospect will be prayerfully "released." Suddenly, he and his beautiful family will be off to another part of the globe. It can be extremely difficult to lose these men (and their families) who were so useful in the church. But the kind of men the church should release are those who will be missed the most.

After submitting to the Spirit's call and experiencing the loving confirmation of the church, Paul and Barnabas were off to Seleucia to catch a ship to Cyprus. The world would never be the same.

Questions for Discussion

1. Have you conversed with or spent time around any missionaries or missionary helpers? Does anything stand out regarding those encounters?

2. We saw that it is technically the Holy Spirit who "sends" missionaries, and the local church "releases" them. Do you think this an important clarification? Why or why not?

3. What various aspects of a man's life should be in place in order to be considered for missions work?

4. Has a missionary ever been sent from your church? Tell the story.

5. What decision-making process is in place in your church in order to cooperate with the Holy Spirit in sending out missionaries?

4 So, being sent out by the Holy Spirit, they went down to Seleucia, and from there they sailed to Cyprus. 5 When they arrived at Salamis, they proclaimed the word of God in the synagogues of the Jews. And they had John to assist them. 6 When they had gone through the whole island as far as Paphos, they came upon a certain magician, a Jewish false prophet named Bar-Jesus. 7 He was with the proconsul, Sergius Paulus, a man of intelligence, who summoned Barnabas and Saul and sought to hear the word of God. 8 But Elymas the magician (for that is the meaning of his name) opposed them, seeking to turn the proconsul away from the faith. 9 But Saul, who was also called Paul, filled with the Holy Spirit, looked intently at him 10 and said, "You son of the devil, you enemy of all righteousness, full of all deceit and villainy, will you not stop making crooked the straight paths of the Lord? 11 And now, behold, the hand of the Lord is upon you, and you will be blind and unable to see the sun for a time." Immediately mist and darkness fell upon him, and he went about seeking people to lead him by the hand. 12 Then the proconsul believed, when he saw what had occurred, for he was astonished at the teaching of the Lord.

Acts 13:4-12

Chapter Three

Priority

Starting location: **Seleucia**

Cities on the journey: **Salamis, Paphos (both on the island of Cyprus)**

Within the first few hours that Adoniram Judson and his wife of seven days, Ann, set sail from America to take the gospel to the East, Ann was overcome by seasickness. She said that on the first night at sea, she "had many distressing apprehensions of death," and, "felt unwilling to die on the sea, not so much on account of my state after death, as the dreadfulness of perishing amid the waves."[11]

And then, before the first week of sailing was over, the ship almost sank because of a leak![12] Soon, life on the ship settled down and the Judson's were able to rest before embarking on one of the most inspiring American missionary endeavors in history.

---

[11] Courtney Anderson, *To the Golden Shore: The Life of Adoniram Judson* (Boston: Little, Brown, and Company, 1956), 125.
[12] Ibid.

We have no record of anything difficult happening as Barnabas and Saul (Paul) sailed southwest over 100 miles from Seleucia, the Mediterranean port of Antioch, to Salamis on the island of Cyprus (a Roman senatorial province since 22 B.C.). We can assume the short journey across the sea was calm. Barnabas, a Cypriot by birth (Acts 4:36), probably knew that there were multiple synagogues in Salamis. I envision these two missionaries talking through potential scenarios, and praying for receptive hearts. The gospel had come to Cyprus previously (cf. 11:19-20), but it was about to arrive again.

Gospel Priority

"When they arrived at Salamis, they proclaimed the word of God in the synagogues of the Jews" (13:5). Not much is documented about the ministry in Salamis, a town on the east coast of Cyprus. What is recorded is noteworthy because it points to the priority of these missionaries: "they proclaimed the word of God," which does not mean that they gave prepared sermons like what happens today in churches on Sunday mornings. Instead, "the word of God" is another way of saying "gospel" (cf. 14:7, 21). They shared God's message, also called "the word of his grace" (14:3), and as they did this in Salamis, "[T]hey had John to assist them" (13:5).

Paul informs us in Colossians 4:10 that John Mark was the cousin of Barnabas. Throughout his ministry, Paul was helped by workers like John Mark, and even sent them on assignment. According to New Testament scholar Eckhard J. Schnabel, Acts and Paul's letters mention thirty-eight such workers under Paul's leadership (approximately 18% were women, typically serving locally).[13]

The specific location of their gospel preaching in Salamis, "the synagogues of the Jews," is connected to redemptive history.

---

[13] *Paul the Missionary*, 248, 250.

This is mentioned with more explanation later in Acts 13 (vv. 44-48), but some comments might be helpful here. Ever since God's covenant with Abraham in Genesis 12, the Jewish nation, as God's chosen people, had a special place in God's plan for salvation history (see Romans 9-11; cf. Matthew 10:5-6; Acts 3:26). This does not mean every Jew who has ever lived will be saved. Paul addressed this idea in Romans 9 when he said that "not all who are descended from Israel belong to Israel" (v. 6). Nevertheless, Paul is adamant that "a remnant of them will be saved" (v. 27). Therefore, God's unique relationship with Israel, and the hope that some Jews would believe, compelled these missionaries to prioritize where they first took the good news (cf. Acts 13:46; Romans 1:16).

It was also highly strategic for these missionaries to find a synagogue meeting wherever they went because those in attendance, both Jews *and Gentiles*, knew the Old Testament and believed in the God it revealed. A major part of synagogue meetings was devoted to hearing Scripture read and taught (cf. Acts 13:15-16). Rulers of a synagogue would ask certain men to speak about what was read, including visitors like Paul whose reputation must have preceded him (or he convinced the synagogue ruler to let him speak). Paul used the Scriptures that they believed to show them that the Christ had to die and rise again, and that Jesus was the Christ (cf. 17:1-3). In some ways, this was "easy" evangelism.

Engaging Present-day Religious Discussions

A similar tactic might be employed today by going into churches that have almost (or entirely) abandoned the gospel.[14] At a minimum, some type of "religious discussion" will be happening.

---

[14] See Jim Elliff, "How Should We Get a Crowd for the Gospel," https://www.ccwtoday.org/2006/04/how-should-we-get-a-crowd-for-the-gospel/, accessed August 13, 2021.

I walked into a progressive church's Sunday School class one morning hoping to get an opportunity to share about Jesus. I told them I was a pastor of a church that meets Sunday evenings, that I love to talk about the Lord and the Bible, and that I desire to encourage local churches in my area. I asked if I could join the class that morning. "Sure!" They were reading a book that was minimally based on the Bible, but I did my best to talk about Scripture with the nine or ten people in attendance. Something remarkable happened at the end of the class: the older lady who was the teacher said, "Would you teach us next week?" That began three years of teaching that Sunday School class, and it seems that two of the ladies in the group (one in her mid-seventies, one in her mid-eighties) were converted during that time!

Not everyone should do this type of evangelism (especially those who may be easily persuaded away from the truth). Yet, for some, it is worth a prayerful attempt. If you think this might be for you, first talk with your pastor(s) to make sure they believe you are ready, but also so that they understand your intentions.

Proclamation or Blueprints?

The big idea to learn from the stop in Salamis is that from the *beginning* of the first missionary journey, *gospel proclamation was the priority*. So to the missionary who is reading this, I would encourage you to reflect on this question: "Is your ministry first of all about preaching the gospel, or have you let other responsibilities exhaust your time and energy?"

In my travels for ministry around the world, I have met well-meaning missionaries who are regularly engaged in "vital ministry projects" such as building construction or curriculum development. I often wonder if before they arrived on the field they envisioned participating so heavily in these types of activities. I am guessing that their initial burden for the nations was all about people coming to Christ. A missionary deeply engaged in blueprint analysis or resource writing might defend himself: "It will facilitate gospel advance!" And so it might, and maybe you *are* supposed to invest deeply in those projects. But perhaps not, because it will keep you from your main responsibility.

Gospel Unstoppability

The missionaries traveled from Salamis and went "through the whole island" (13:6), probably on the southern road that passed through Kition, Amathus, and Kourion. It was a further trip of approximately 100 miles to the western side of the island of Cyprus and the city of Paphos, the capital and governmental center of the province. Once there, they met the highest ranking Roman official on the island, "Sergius Paulus," who was "the proconsul" (governor; v. 7). He was "a man of intelligence, who summoned Barnabas and Saul and sought to hear the word of God" (v. 7). Somehow he had heard that these missionaries had a message from God, and he wanted to hear what they had to say.

However, Satan *hates* the progress of the gospel, so standing next to Sergius Paulus was "a certain magician, a Jewish false prophet named Bar-Jesus" (v. 6), also called "Elymas the magician (for that is the meaning of his name)" (v. 8a). He was probably something like a sorcerer who interpreted dreams and predicted the future, supposedly providing knowledge of divine activity. He advised the proconsul with this "talent." His position in Sergius Paulus' court presumably made him popular and wealthy, so he instantly sensed a potential disruption to his life of luxury when he heard the proconsul call for the missionaries. He had to act. Once the missionaries arrived, Elymas "opposed them, seeking to turn the proconsul away from the faith" (v. 8b).

Luke records a stern confrontation: "But Saul, who was also called Paul, filled with the Holy Spirit, looked intently at him and said, 'You son of the devil, you enemy of all righteousness, full of all deceit and villainy, will you not stop making crooked the straight paths of the Lord?'" (vv. 9-10). His name was "Bar-Jesus" ("son of salvation"), but he behaved deceptively, wickedly, and Satanically (thus, the "son of the devil" designation) to keep the salvation of the Lord from coming "straight" (v. 10) to the palace of Paulus.

At this point in the story, Luke mentioned another name for Saul. "Saul" was his Hebrew name, but now that he was preaching the gospel in predominantly Gentile locations, Luke began using a Roman name that he would have been called — "Paul." From this point on not only in the first journey, but also in Acts, Paul is presented as the prominent leader.

Paul was not finished talking to Elymas, but proceeded to predict a temporary judgment upon him which quickly materialized.

> "And now behold, the hand of the Lord is upon you, and you will be blind and unable to see the sun for a time." Immediately mist and darkness fell upon him, and he went about seeking people to lead him by the hand. (v. 11)

Satan vs. the Holy Spirit

Even though the narrative focuses especially on two *physical* beings, Elymas and Paul, behind each stood powerful *spiritual* beings — the devil and the Holy Spirit. Here is an obvious implication for today: as the gospel advances, it will be met by opposition that is not only in a natural realm, but a spiritual realm in which Satan and his demons operate (see Ephesians 6:12). Satan despises God, his purposes, his people, and his missionaries, and he works tirelessly to keep people from coming under Christ's loving rule.

But here's the encouraging truth for missionaries and anyone who wants to see the gospel embraced by unbelievers: Satan cannot stop the progress of the gospel *because the Holy Spirit loves the advance of the gospel and makes sure that it happens.* In this first missionary journey, the Holy Spirit's role was central, first in sending the missionaries (13:2, 4), and then in Paphos where Paul was able to speak to Elymas with boldness and prophetic certainty because he was "filled with the Holy Spirit" (v. 9). And though we do not have all of the details, how did these two unknown missionaries ever get an audience with the ruler of the whole island? Even if there were human mechanisms involved, we must conclude this was ultimately a rescue mission of the Holy Spirit who was revealing to these missionaries from the start that they had no one to fear, not even Satan himself, as they moved out to the "end of the earth" (Acts 1:8). The gospel was always their priority, and it was unstoppable. The lost will be found. Even a prominent, seemingly unreachable Gentile ruler can be converted if that is what God wants!

What happened in Paphos? "Then the proconsul believed, when he saw what had occurred, for he was astonished at the teaching of the Lord" (13:12). Once he saw Elymas struck blind, Sergius Paulus trusted in Christ. A Jewish man who was determined to keep the proconsul from believing ironically became the instrument through which the good news was authenticated. This led to the Gentile Sergius Paulus being amazed at the gospel, and then believing in Jesus. What an encouragement this must have been to these missionaries at the beginning of their journey. If the Holy Spirit is present, the gospel can go anywhere and save anyone!

Then and Now

The experience and ministry of the missions team on the island of Cyprus can be summarized in three statements.

1. Gospel proclamation was foundational.
2. Satanic opposition was inevitable.
3. The gospel was unstoppable.

Nothing has changed for missionaries today, or for any believer who longs to see people saved. Proclaim the gospel, expect Satanic opposition, and know that Satan is no match for the Holy Spirit who *will* advance the gospel when he determines. Count on it!

It was true at Paphos.

It was true also for Dr. William Leslie, a missionary to the Congo, who ministered there seventeen years and then was asked to leave by tribal leaders. He left thinking he had failed, and he died nine years after arriving home. Yet eighty-four years later, a ministry team went back to the remote area where Leslie ministered and the group was startled to discover a flourishing network of churches.[15] The gospel could not be stopped.

That will be true in your life as well, as you faithfully proclaim Jesus.

The gospel was powerful on the island of Cyprus, but it was time for the missionaries to depart. Others needed to hear the good news. As the story unfolds, Luke not only tells what happened in the next location, he also reveals the content of the message Paul proclaimed. It is as if we get to sit in a synagogue meeting and hear the good news straight from the apostle's mouth!

---

[15] Mark Ellis, "Missionary Died Thinking He was a Failure; 84 Years Later Thriving Churches Found Hidden in the Jungle," https://godreports.com/2014/05/missionary-died-thinking-he-was-a-failure-84-years-later-thriving-churches-found-hidden-in-the-jungle/, accessed June 13, 2020.

Questions for Discussion

1. Have you ever been in a religious setting where you suspected you were the only believer (funeral, visiting a church with a friend or relative, campus ministry, etc.)? What did you hear? How did you feel?

2. Would it be wise for you to go into a church without the gospel (or other settings where discussions about God and Scripture are happening) in order to evangelize? Why or why not?

3. Do you think very often about Satanic opposition to gospel advance? Talk about it.

4. What hope does the Spirit's role in gospel advancement give you?

13 Now Paul and his companions set sail from Paphos and came to Perga in Pamphylia. And John left them and returned to Jerusalem, 14 but they went on from Perga and came to Antioch in Pisidia. And on the Sabbath day they went into the synagogue and sat down. 15 After the reading from the Law and the Prophets, the rulers of the synagogue sent a message to them, saying, "Brothers, if you have any word of encouragement for the people, say it." 16 So Paul stood up, and motioning with his hand said:

"Men of Israel and you who fear God, listen. 17 The God of this people Israel chose our fathers and made the people great during their stay in the land of Egypt, and with uplifted arm he led them out of it. 18 And for about forty years he put up with them in the wilderness. 19 And after destroying seven nations in the land of Canaan, he gave them their land as an inheritance. 20 All this took about 450 years. And after that he gave them judges until Samuel the prophet. 21 Then they asked for a king, and God gave them Saul the son of Kish, a man of the tribe of Benjamin, for forty years. 22 And when he had removed him, he raised up David to be their king, of whom he testified and said, 'I have found in David the son of Jesse a man after my heart, who will do all my will.' 23 Of this man's offspring God has brought to Israel a Savior, Jesus, as he promised. 24 Before his coming, John had proclaimed a baptism of repentance to all the people of Israel. 25 And as John was finishing his course, he said, 'What do you suppose that I am? I am not he. No, but behold, after me one is coming, the sandals of whose feet I am not worthy to untie.'"

Acts 13:13-25

Chapter Four

Message

Starting location: **Paphos**

Cities on the journey: **Perga, Pisidian Antioch**

If we did not have Acts in our Bibles, we would transition from John's Gospel to Romans and ask, "Who is this man named Paul who calls himself an apostle?" Acts fills in an abundance of critical details about not only Paul, but numerous individuals and churches in the remainder of the New Testament. For example, the story of the first missionary journey in Acts 13-14 includes Paul's ministry in Galatia. The churches he started there are likely the recipients of the letter we call "Galatians," written by Paul once he returned to Antioch in Syria.

Acts also provides several examples of the content of the gospel that the early church proclaimed. In our study through Acts 13-14, we have come to a section that includes the message that Paul gave in a synagogue in Pisidian Antioch (13:16-41). Even though the word Paul shared was directed especially to "Men of Israel" and "those who fear God" (i.e., Gentiles who worshipped Israel's God), this is a message for everyone.

The Journey to Pisidian Antioch

Paul and his team left the island of Paphos and sailed northwest on the Mediterranean Sea approximately 150 miles to the coast of south central Asia Minor (modern Turkey), eventually arriving at "Perga in Pamphylia" (v. 13a) about ten miles inland. It would have been accessed either by foot once porting in Attalia, or via the Cestrus River which passed by Perga.

At this point, no mention is made of preaching in Perga (though see 14:25). However, from there, "John left them and returned to Jerusalem" (13:13b). No reason is given for his departure. We assume this was a tense moment on the journey because of the dispute Paul and Barnabas had about John Mark prior to the second missionary journey (see 15:36-41). That disagreement was so severe that they ended up parting ways (vv. 39-40).

Back to the first journey. John Mark did not keep going, but the gospel did. The majority of atlases depict Paul and Barnabas traveling on a mostly northward route through the snow-capped Taurus mountains and eventually around the southeast edge of Lake Limnai before finally arriving at Pisidian Antioch. However, Bible archeology scholar Mark Wilson makes a compelling case that Paul and Barnabas probably took the Roman road called the Via Sebaste (traveling approximately 156 miles from Perga to Antioch).[16] From Perga, this road went significantly northwest around the western side of Lake Ascanius, and then northeast under snowcapped Mount Gelinick before passing along the northwest portion of Lake Limnai, and then finally ascended the foothills up to Pisidian Antioch. Wilson notes, "While 37% longer than the

---

[16] "The Route of Paul's First Journey to Pisidian Antioch," https://www.sevenchurches.org/wp-content/uploads/2020/03/Route-of-Pauls-First-Journey-Wilson-NTS.pdf, accessed December 9, 2020. This article originally appeared in *New Testament Studies*, vol. 55, Issue 4 (United Kingdom: Cambridge Press, 2009), 471-483.

central route, it was much easier because it avoided the deep valleys and difficult terrain of the Taurus Mountains," and it was also "probably the safest route."[17]

The Via Sebaste, built in 6 B.C. during the time of Augustus, was "paved" according to first-century standards. Historian Edwin M. Yamauchi notes that these roads "were generally 10 to 12 feet wide," and then he quotes Plutarch to explain how they were constructed.

> "The roads were carried through the country in a perfectly straight line, and were paved with hewn stone and reinforced with banks of tight-rammed sand. Depressions were filled up, all intersecting torrents or ravines were bridged, and both sides were of equal and corresponding height, so that the work presented everywhere an even and beautiful appearance."[18]

Unless you were a government official or in the cavalry, you would likely have traveled on these roads by foot, not horse, walking about twenty miles a day (three per hour).[19]

After a long walk over a number of days, the missionaries finally arrived in "Antioch in Pisidia" (13:14) within the Roman province of Galatia. Technically, Antioch was "close to" Pisidia, not literally within that region. Eckhard J. Schnabel explains.

> The phrase "Antioch in Pisidia" in Acts 13:14 does not assert that Antioch was actually located in the region of Pisidia: the city belonged to Phrygia. The appellation "Pisidian" distinguishes this Antioch from another city named Antioch that was situated on the Maeander River and was also located in Phrygia.[20]

---

[17] Ibid.
[18] "On the Road With Paul," https://christianhistoryinstitute.org/magazine/article/on-the-road-with-paul, accessed August 31, 2021.
[19] Ibid.
[20] *Paul the Missionary*, 79.

To speak of "Antioch in Pisidia" or "Pisidian Antioch" (my preference) also helps us not to confuse it with Antioch in Syria (Syrian Antioch), the city from which Paul and Barnabas were sent.

Luke does not tell us why Paul and Barnabas chose to visit this town, though some have speculated that they went there because Sergius Paulus, recently converted in Paphos on the island of Cyprus (13:6-12), urged the missionaries to take the gospel to that influential city because he had relatives there.[21] It is noteworthy that Paul says in Galatians, "You know that it was because of a bodily ailment that I preached the gospel to you at first" (4:13). There might have been a medical reason (better climate? expert care?) for the trip to Pisdian Antioch some 3,500 feet above sea level. We may someday find out that Sergius Paulus reasoned with Paul, "Antioch would be a perfect climate for you to recover physically. And I can get word to my family to receive you and give you a place to stay. I would be so delighted if they got to hear the good news from you!"

The Message in Pisidian Antioch

Once they arrived in Pisidian Antioch and settled in, it was time to preach the good news about Jesus.

> And on the Sabbath day they went into the synagogue and sat down. After the reading from the Law and the Prophets, the rulers of the synagogue sent a message to them, saying, "Brothers, if you have any word of encouragement for the people, say it." So Paul stood up, and motioning with his hand said:
> "Men of Israel and you who fear God, listen." (13:14b-16)

---

[21] Peterson, *Acts*, 385.

Preacher and Audience

As mentioned in chapter 3, it was common for synagogue officials to ask visiting Jewish men who had a reputation for teaching to share a "word of encouragement" that would both explain and apply the Scripture readings just given. Paul possibly received this opportunity to exhort because he was "educated at the feet of Gamaliel" (22:3) and a revered Pharisee (5:34). The apostle, perhaps seated on a stone seat found along the tiered synagogue wall, gladly took this invitation to address a group of people which included both Jews and Gentiles ("you who fear God").[22]

Exhortation

Put simply, Paul urged his listeners to respond to the gospel by communicating to them that *salvation was possible and urgently important because the promised Savior, Jesus, had come.*

Part I

In the first part of Paul's "word of encouragement" (vv. 17-25), he demonstrated that *God's gracious dealings with Israel in the past led to the arrival of the promised Savior, Jesus.* He started with familiar territory for his listeners by recounting in chronological fashion the record of God sovereignly and graciously acting on Israel's behalf. They were God's chosen people, and even though they routinely behaved wickedly, he was gracious to them — delivering them out of slavery to the Egyptians, providing for them in the wilderness, granting them the land he promised, sending judges to deliver them, and giving them kings including David, "a man after [God's] heart" (v. 22).

---

[22] God-fearers are also addressed in verse 26, but then "devout converts to Judaism" are mentioned in verse 43. So it seems that Gentiles who had not yet fully converted to Judaism (by submitting to circumcision) and Gentiles who were full converts to Judaism were present in the synagogue.

Once he mentioned David, it was time to tell them about the one to whom all of Israel's history and all of God's grace was pointing: "Of this man's offspring God has brought to Israel a Savior, Jesus, as he promised" (v. 23). The Lord promised David a son who would reign eternally (2 Samuel 7:12-13). Jesus was this son sent purposefully to save his people, the royal heir who would sit eternally on the throne of David.

At this point, Paul reminded them about John the Baptist's ministry (vv. 24-25). Why? John's ministry communicated what all of Israel's history pointed to: Jesus is the center and climax of redemptive history!

Paul's message has two more parts to it. We will get to those in the next chapter.

However, we should pause at this point and consider what Paul's exhortation is revealing to us about God: He is sovereign over history, and he is amazingly gracious! God would have been just to give to each of us an eternal, excruciating, and well-deserved punishment. He did not have to send his Son. He did not have to order time and events such that the center of history would be the ministry of his Son on behalf of sinners. But that is exactly what he did.

This is good news for the world. This is good news for *you*. This is a message worth carrying to the nations regardless of the cost!

Questions for Discussion

1. Was there anything interesting or new to you regarding the way Paul and Barnabas got from one place to the next?

2. Describe a time when you heard the gospel faithfully preached to unbelievers. What made it memorable?

3. Read 2 Samuel 7:12-17 and Luke 1:30-33. How do these verses relate to Acts 13:22-23?

4. Does God's sovereignty over history trouble you or excite you? Why?

26 "Brothers, sons of the family of Abraham, and those among you who fear God, to us has been sent the message of this salvation. 27 For those who live in Jerusalem and their rulers, because they did not recognize him nor understand the utterances of the prophets, which are read every Sabbath, fulfilled them by condemning him. 28 And though they found in him no guilt worthy of death, they asked Pilate to have him executed. 29 And when they had carried out all that was written of him, they took him down from the tree and laid him in a tomb. 30 But God raised him from the dead, 31 and for many days he appeared to those who had come up with him from Galilee to Jerusalem, who are now his witnesses to the people. 32 And we bring you the good news that what God promised to the fathers, 33 this he has fulfilled to us their children by raising Jesus, as also it is written in the second Psalm, "'You are my Son, today I have begotten you.' 34 And as for the fact that he raised him from the dead, no more to return to corruption, he has spoken in this way, "'I will give you the holy and sure blessings of David.' 35 Therefore he says also in another psalm,"'You will not let your Holy One see corruption.' 36 For David, after he had served the purpose of God in his own generation, fell asleep and was laid with his fathers and saw corruption, 37 but he whom God raised up did not see corruption.

38 Let it be known to you therefore, brothers, that through this man forgiveness of sins is proclaimed to you, 39 and by him everyone who believes is freed from everything from which you could not be freed by the law of Moses. 40 Beware, therefore, lest what is said in the Prophets should come about: 41 "'Look, you scoffers, be astounded and perish; for I am doing a work in your days, a work that you will not believe, even if one tells it to you.'"

Acts 13:26-41

Chapter Five

Message (continued)

Starting location: **Pisidian Antioch**

Cities on the journey: **Pisidian Antioch**

I embarrassed myself in a Bible study of a church mostly void of the gospel. I went to this gathering because I wanted to tell the group around the table what they probably did not want to hear, that Jesus is Lord of all. But then I dropped my pen on the floor. No big deal, right? Wrong! As I leaned down to pick it up, I accidentally, and with some force, brushed the back side of the lady sitting next to me. Yikes! And then, before I could get the "I'm so sorry" out of my mouth, as I raised up I struck my head forcefully on the table. The bang and vibration were a distraction to all, and everyone looked at me as if to say, "Who is this guy, why is he here, and what is his problem!" I did not say much the rest of the study.

Paul's experience in the synagogue in Pisidian Antioch was the polar opposite of mine that fateful Sunday. In the last chapter, we followed Paul and Barnabas from the island of

Cyprus across the Mediterranean Sea to "Perga in Pamphylia" and finally to Pisidian Antioch (13:13-14). It was in that city that Paul was asked to give a "word of encouragement" in the synagogue (v. 15), and he models for us courage, clarity, and in some ways a timeless strategy in addressing lost people with the gospel. As mentioned in chapter 4, Paul's goal was to tell those in attendance that *salvation was possible and urgently important because the promised Savior, Jesus, had come.*

Exhortation

Part I (review)

In the first part of his message (vv.17-25), Paul reflected on God's sovereignty and kindness in his previous associations with Israel. God's grace toward Israel in the past was preparation for the arrival of the promised Davidic son, Jesus, who would save his people. In summary, Paul began by communicating this: *God's gracious dealings with Israel in the past led to the arrival of the promised Savior, Jesus* (vv. 17-25).

Part II

If part one was about *past* grace leading to the Savior, in part two (vv. 26-37) Paul emphasized to his listeners that this grace, this Savior, was for them *in the present*. We might title this part of Paul's message like this: *the message of this salvation has already come to us, and here's the evidence.* Verse 27 begins with the important word "for," indicating Paul sought to prove that "the message of this salvation" had been sent to them (as he had just stated in v. 26).

Put simply, Paul showed that what was prophesied about Jesus had been fulfilled. He was rejected by many in Jerusalem, leading to his death, but his crucifixion, and subsequent resurrection, were accomplished just as had been promised. "The message of this salvation" was now what they all were hearing and considering that day in the synagogue.

And we bring you the good news that what God promised to the fathers, this he has fulfilled to us their children by raising Jesus. (vv. 32-33a)

In order to support his argument, Paul pointed to three Old Testament texts which allude to David but were fulfilled by the resurrection of Christ — Psalm 2:7; Isaiah 55:3; and Psalm 16:10.

Part III

Paul was not only interested in the past (vv. 17-25) and the present (vv. 26-37), but also the future, in particular the eternal state of his hearers. So in the third part of his message (vv. 38-41), Paul essentially said this: *belief in Jesus brings forgiveness and justification, but rejection brings judgment.* This was an unexpected, remarkable moment in the synagogue that day as Paul's word of exhortation turned into a plea to come to Christ.

There is a phrase from modern day golf tournaments that might help us to understand what Paul was saying in this concluding section of his message, and also how he was going against proper synagogue etiquette. The Masters is an annual golf tournament in which the greatest golfers in the world play for one of the most coveted trophies in the sport. The competition is held at Augusta National Golf Course in Augusta, Georgia, and there is a certain decorum that is expected of those who attend. Here's a sample of what tournament officials say is the proper etiquette.

> In exchange for the privilege of viewing one of golf's greatest spectacles it is anticipated that you will act courteously and display equal encouragement to all participants. Bad manners will not be tolerated. You should be quiet when silence is required, remain stationary while a shot is being executed and adhere to instructions by officials. Players should never be accosted even if they are acquaintances. Any excessive noise or shouting (e.g. You're the man!, etc.) will not be tolerated and may result in dismissal.[23]

In this final part of his message, Paul seemed to be ignoring what might have been considered appropriate "synagogue etiquette" and was boldly declaring, "Jesus is the man!" He's "the man" because of who he is as David's promised son; he's "the man" because he is the risen Savior. Therefore, this had immediate implications practically and personally for every sinner (everyone!) in the synagogue.

> Let it be known to you therefore, brothers, that through this man forgiveness of sins is proclaimed to you, and by him everyone who believes is freed [that is, "justified," meaning declared righteous in God's sight] from everything from which you could not be freed [justified] by the law of Moses. (vv. 38-39)

Paul's listeners thought they could be right with God through obedience to the law of Moses. "Not a chance!" Paul declares. The law only brings condemnation and death. Paul would later say in Galatians that "a person is not justified by works of the law" (Galatians 2:16). Their only hope of forgiveness of sins and their only assurance of justification was through the merits of Jesus. They needed to believe in Jesus the Christ who took their sins on the cross. In exchange they would have his perfect, righteous life credited to their account.

---

[23] "Augusta National Golf Course Etiquette," https://www.executivemarketing.net/etiquette.cfm, accessed August 13, 2021.

It is true that the emphasis in the preaching of the gospel in Acts is the resurrection and Lordship of Jesus. But we see in Paul's final plea that Christ's resurrection and Lordship means something wonderful regarding man's greatest need: a person can have his sins forgiven; an individual can be reconciled to God. But it's only possible through the one who is "the man."

> Not the labor of my hands
> Can fulfill Thy law's demands.
> Could my zeal no respite know,
> Could my tears forever flow;
> All for sin could not atone;
> Thou must save,
> And thou alone.[24]

Paul then warned his listeners in verses 40-41 by quoting Habakkuk 1:5, which told Judah of the judgment that God would bring on them through the force of the Babylonians because of their lack of repentance. The implication for those in Pisidian Antioch? Just as God poured out his wrath *then*, so he would on *them* if they rejected this Savior. Their response to Jesus Christ determined their eternal state.

Our Response

You have heard Paul's message, also. Now what?

Believe

First, if you have not yet believed, what are you waiting for? Remarkably, "to us has been sent the message of this salvation." Paul was saying that to his listeners in Pisidian Antioch, but it is true for you as well.

---

[24] "Rock of Ages," words by Augustus M. Toplady. Public Domain.

Whether you have ever been under the law of Moses or not, the message is still for us all: justification does not come through adherence to an outward religious system, even if it is a law which God gave! Justification is only possible by faith in Christ alone. Rest in Christ, believing that what he accomplished through his substitutionary death and resurrection is sufficient to deliver you from sin's penalty and grip on your life.

I have a friend who served in the army as a lieutenant colonel and green beret. He sometimes even rubbed shoulders with the famed "Seal Team Six." During lunch one day, I was probing him for details of his adventures, and he made a comment about the military's special ops, sharing something like this: "If we decide we are going to kill some notorious leader around the world like Osama Bin Laden, it's not a matter *if* we will do it, it's only a matter of *when*." In other words, for those wicked leaders, judgment was guaranteed. The same goes for sinners in the hands of a righteously angry God — it's not a matter *if* he will pour out his wrath upon you, it's only a matter of *when* . . . unless you flee to the risen Christ, believe he paid the penalty on the cross in your place, and shift your allegiance to him.

Tell

Second, Jesus is the center and theme of the message that saves. Keep telling others about him. Do not give up on his story. If you are a believer, it is, after all, the good news about Christ that saved you! I am often inspired to keep sharing the gospel with the lost by the memory that a no-name high school basketball coach in the middle of the cornfields in Ohio told me about Jesus, and it changed my eternity.

Send carefully

Third, make sure that every missionary you send eagerly and often proclaims the gospel *before he goes*. So far in the first missionary journey, we have seen that Paul was fervid in gospel proclamation, but this was nothing new — from the moment of his conversion (over a decade before this message in Pisidian Antioch), Paul was highly evangelistic (cf. Acts 9:20-22, 28-29).

Those you send out must already demonstrate a pattern of evangelizing. If they are not known for that "at home," they almost certainly will not change once they are looking in the eyes of someone who does not even speak their language, and who has strange and possibly chilling ideas about humanity and "spirits" and the life to come.

Because Paul's message in the synagogue in Pisidian Antioch covers so much space in Acts 13-14, Luke (and the Holy Spirit) obviously thought we should spend a good amount of time reflecting on it. In the next chapter, we will follow the narrative as it shifts to the fascinating and varied responses of the people, both Jews and, most dramatically, Gentiles. Joy and the Holy Spirit were filling the nations!

Questions for Discussion

1. Are there any elements in Paul's message in the synagogue that need to be emphasized more in evangelism today?

2. What does it mean to "believe" in Jesus?

3. Do you have anyone you regularly tell about Jesus? How has it been going lately?

4. Who are your church's missionaries? Where are they located? What stories do you recall of their evangelistic efforts?

42 As they went out, the people begged that these things might be told them the next Sabbath. 43 And after the meeting of the synagogue broke up, many Jews and devout converts to Judaism followed Paul and Barnabas, who, as they spoke with them, urged them to continue in the grace of God.

44 The next Sabbath almost the whole city gathered to hear the word of the Lord. 45 But when the Jews saw the crowds, they were filled with jealousy and began to contradict what was spoken by Paul, reviling him. 46 And Paul and Barnabas spoke out boldly, saying, "It was necessary that the word of God be spoken first to you. Since you thrust it aside and judge yourselves unworthy of eternal life, behold, we are turning to the Gentiles. 47 For so the Lord has commanded us, saying, "'I have made you a light for the Gentiles, that you may bring salvation to the ends of the earth.'"

48 And when the Gentiles heard this, they began rejoicing and glorifying the word of the Lord, and as many as were appointed to eternal life believed. 49 And the word of the Lord was spreading throughout the whole region. 50 But the Jews incited the devout women of high standing and the leading men of the city, stirred up persecution against Paul and Barnabas, and drove them out of their district. 51 But they shook off the dust from their feet against them and went to Iconium. 52 And the disciples were filled with joy and with the Holy Spirit.

Acts 13:42-52

Chapter Six

Response

Starting location: **Pisidian Antioch**

Cities on the journey: **Pisidian Antioch, Iconium**

As a young pastor in a church that had multiple splits before I arrived, I quickly learned a valuable lesson: *When the gospel is proclaimed, people will respond.* People rejoice, or are curious, or frustrated, or bored, or angry. But there are really only two responses: acceptance or rejection; faith in Christ or refusal to submit to Christ.

This is how it's always been with the gospel. The apostle Paul was in a synagogue meeting in Pisidian Antioch when he was given the opportunity to proclaim the good news (Acts 13:13-41). The attendees not only included Jews, but also Gentiles (vv. 16, 26, 43). The gospel was preached, but then what happened? As always, people responded.

Positive Responses

The first response to Paul's preaching is in verse 42: "As they went out, the people begged that these things might be told them the next Sabbath." We might wonder why Paul did not say to those asking for more, "Okay, you want to hear what else I have to say? Gather around again." But he was satisfied that the gospel was already proclaimed.

"And after the meeting of the synagogue broke up, many Jews and devout converts to Judaism[25] followed Paul and Barnabas, who, as they spoke with them, urged them to continue in the grace of God" (v. 43). It is difficult to know for sure, but it seems that these individuals had been converted, especially since they were exhorted to "continue in the grace of God." The word translated "continue" is used elsewhere in Acts in reference to believers, such as 11:23 (translated "remain faithful") where Luke says Barnabas encouraged the new believers in Antioch (in Syria) to "remain faithful to the Lord with steadfast purpose."

So here in Pisdian Antioch, these people had heard about the "grace of God" in Christ, specifically that forgiveness of sins and acceptance with God was gained not by law-keeping, but through faith in God's Son. It was this message that they were told to keep believing.

During the next week, Paul's message in the synagogue was apparently the subject of much conversation throughout the primarily Gentile city of Antioch. On the next Sabbath, the interest of the crowd was intense and the size demanding because "almost the whole city gathered to hear the word of the Lord" (v. 44).

---

[25] No mention is made of God-fearing Gentiles being present at this point, just those who were full converts to Judaism.

A Negative Response

Not all of the responses were positive: "But when the Jews saw the crowds, they were filled with jealousy and began to contradict what was spoken by Paul, reviling him" (v. 45). Why the jealousy? It was because Paul dared to say that the Messiah had already been on earth, had come not only to save Jews, but Gentiles, and that a person is granted entrance into the Messiah's kingdom by faith alone. There was no need to first become a Jew.

This was a highly compelling idea to the Gentiles present. But the Jews "began to contradict" the message and slander the messenger (v. 45). This only emboldened the missionaries. It is at this point in the story that something major transpired: gospel proclamation efforts shifted exclusively to the Gentiles in Pisidian Antioch, resulting in many conversions and gospel advance (v. 49). Here, then, in Pisidian Antioch was the first major gospel outreach *exclusively* to a large number of Gentiles in one location.

This does not mean that Paul was done preaching the gospel to his fellow Jews. In the next city on the journey, Iconium, Paul again went "into the Jewish synagogue and spoke in such a way that a great number of both Jews and Gentiles believed" (14:1). Paul continued to affirm, as he said in Antioch, that "it was necessary that the word of God be spoken first" to Jews (13:46). Israel had a unique place in redemptive history as God's chosen people who were to live under his rule and be a blessing to the nations (Genesis 12:1-3). They failed, but God's promise to Israel of deliverance through a Messiah remained. Since Jesus was *their* promised Messiah, Paul took the message to the Jew first (cf. Romans 1:16-17). But now, in this city, these Jews had rejected the gospel, judging themselves "unworthy of eternal life;" they had deliberately disqualified themselves, essentially saying that they had no need of this Savior. Because of that rejection, the missionaries' focus shifted to the Gentiles (v. 46).

Extremely Positive Responses

Paul's decision to turn to the Gentiles was based on Scripture.

> For so the Lord has commanded us, saying,
> "I have made you a light for the Gentiles, that you may bring salvation to the ends of the earth." (v. 47)

He quoted Isaiah 49:6, which falls within the "Servant" section of Isaiah. Originally, the nation of Israel was to be a "light for the Gentiles," pointing the nations to their God and the salvation that he brings. They failed to fulfill this responsibility, but the Servant Jesus Christ did not. When Jesus was a baby, Simeon took him in his arms and, referencing Isaiah 49:6, declared that he would be "a light for revelation to the Gentiles" (Luke 2:32). And now, remarkably, Paul quotes Isaiah 49:6 and says it applies to him and Barnabas! How is this possible? The Servant of Isaiah, Jesus, has his servants, and in this instance it was Paul and Barnabas who were taking the message of salvation to the Gentiles — the nations. Jesus was still the one proclaiming the good news, but he was doing it through these missionaries (cf. Acts 22:16-18, 22-23).

What happened next? "And when the Gentiles heard this, they began rejoicing and glorifying the word of the Lord, and as many as were appointed to eternal life believed" (Acts 13:48). Too often this verse is only talked about as it relates to the concept of election (God choosing, in eternity past, some to be saved). But that misses the emphasis of this verse within the story. The major point is that when Paul referenced Isaiah 49 about the salvation of Gentiles, this sounded glorious to a group of listening Gentiles. "This is incredible! How wonderful is God's word! Even we Gentiles may be saved!" And then some Gentiles, those whom God had chosen long ago, believed.

So the concept of God appointing some to eternal life is not inserted here primarily to help us understand God's sovereignty and man's responsibility in salvation; it is included to emphasize the marvelous truth that God had Gentiles — the nations — in his heart before the foundation of the earth. This radically changed some Gentiles' lives, evidenced by their immediate desire to tell others in villages "throughout the whole region" about this Savior of the world (v. 49).

Further Negative Responses

The unbelieving Jews in Antioch were incensed, so they brought in the heavy hitters and increased the persecution dramatically: "But the Jews incited the devout women of high standing and the leading men of the city, stirred up persecution against Paul and Barnabas, and drove them out of their district" (v. 50). This time, the missionaries had to go. "But," before they left, "they shook off the dust from their feet against them and went to Iconium" (v. 51). Jesus had instructed his apostles to do this when he sent them out to proclaim the arrival of God's kingdom (Luke 9:5; cf. 10:11). It seems that in Paul's use of this gesture, it was related to what was common for a Jew who, when leaving an "unclean" Gentile territory, would shake the dust from his sandals as a symbol of ridding himself of the "pagan filth" of the place he was leaving. But here in Antioch, Paul and Barnabas, Jews, were shaking off the dust *against fellow Jews,* symbolically declaring *them* spiritually unclean, unbelievers worthy of God's judgment.

But Paul and Barnabas did not only leave behind enemies of God in Pisidian Antioch: "And the disciples were filled with joy and with the Holy Spirit" (v. 52). Some in that city had experienced God's grace in Christ. From day one as new believers, they were living in a city that despised Jesus and his followers. But the Spirit of God within them produced a joy that could not be suppressed.

What About Today?

With the Pisidian Antioch story in mind, think about the proclaimed gospel in the present day and what is *still* true regarding responses to it.

Captivating

First, the gospel is still captivating. It is the story of the most intriguing man who has ever lived, Jesus Christ. It makes sense of the history of humanity and our broken relationship with God, showing the way to be forgiven of sins and reconciled to the Lord. It points to the judgment to come, and the way to be saved from it. It is a message that helps people answer "meaning of life" questions like, "Why am I here?" and "What is wrong with this world?" and "What is wrong with me?" and "Where is history headed?" The gospel continues to enthrall, but even more, it continues to redeem; it's the message that raises the dead; it causes people to hate their sin and love Jesus; it makes people who formerly gloried in wickedness now choose righteousness.

Neither missionaries on the frontlines nor believers in a country that has had the gospel for centuries should question the gospel's power to engage and save. And you do not even have to be very articulate to share it. I am guessing that the majority of us were converted through fairly average gospel presentations, but the truth was there, and our lives were changed forever.

James Alexander Stewart was an evangelist in the first half of the 1900s, and the Lord shockingly provided him with a "co-evangelist" named Herbert Brown who almost always stuttered, except when he was praying! Brown preached to crowds occasionally, but typically his stammering produced a spray of saliva for all to see and even feel if too close.

Nevertheless, God used this awkward preacher. Stewart was speaking of Herbert Brown's preaching when he wrote, "The Spirit of God drove home the words in power. Nobody ever forgot a message of his, for when he sent them to Calvary or hell, it was with great reiteration!"

One Sunday, Stewart had six speaking engagements, but forgot one. Herbert Brown was there, though, and when he came home, Stewart asked him who had preached. Brown responded, "I, of course. We had a great time. The hall was crowded and souls were saved." [26]

Infuriating

Second, the gospel is still infuriating. Some people are too proud to think that they need to be saved. They have been told all of their lives how wonderful they are, and that they can live a fulfilling life if they look within and discover their inherent awesomeness. Others rest in religious practices or general niceness as their path to acceptance with God. The gospel decimates all such thinking. Some will simply walk away when their need for Jesus is proclaimed, but others will stay and fight with lies, contradictions, and maybe even physical assaults.

Paul would eventually be back in Antioch and remind the believers there that "through many tribulations we must enter the kingdom of God" (14:22). Certainly the same remains true for Christ's followers today (cf. 2 Timothy 3:12). We should expect opposition, and it should encourage us when it comes for right reasons (not because you are being a jerk online, for example). Opposition is an indication that we are remaining faithful.

---

[26] This story and these quotes are found in a booklet by James Alexander Stewart, *He Was a Stutterer: The Story of Herbert Brown of England—A Mighty Intercessor* (Asheville, NC: Revival Literature, 2007).

Far-reaching

Third, the gospel is still far-reaching. In other words, the gospel remains a message for the nations. The story of the gospel coming to Pisidian Antioch reminds us that God's *word* has always pointed toward salvation coming to the world (Isaiah 49:6), and God's *heart* has always been for the nations because he elected some Gentiles in eternity past (Acts 13:48). The gospel is a message that people all over the world need, and some *will* embrace it.

This is even happening in recent decades in seemingly "impossible to reach" places like Iran. In an article titled, "Worth a Thousand Years of Waiting: The Staggering Rise of the Church in Iran," Afshin Ziafat says that in Iran, "[M]ore Iranians have become Christians in the last twenty years than in the previous 1,300 years, since Islam came to Iran."[27] Jesus promised to build his church (Matthew 16:18), and he is keeping his word all over the world.

There should be no doubt this far into our study that the gospel is as relevant today as in the first century, and it is as powerful right now, wherever you are in the world, as it was in Paul's day. Not all responses will be favorable; persecution is inevitable. However, singer and songwriter Andrew Peterson reminds us of the gospel's potency in the following words.

> Do you feel the world is broken?
> *We do.*
>
> Do you feel the shadows deepen?
> *We do.*

---

[27] https://www.desiringgod.org/articles/worth-a-thousand-years-of-waiting, accessed July 25, 2020.

But do you know that all the dark won't stop the light from getting through?
We do.[28]

Next we will travel with the missionaries to Iconium where the story will sound familiar, but with a few subtle and critical differences.

---

[28] "Is He Worthy," Words and Music by Andrew Peterson and Ben Shive © 2018 Capitol CMG Genesis (ASCAP) / Vamos Publishing (ASCAP) (Adm. at CapitolCMGPublishing.com) / Jakedog Music (ASCAP) (adm. by MusicServices.org) / Junkbox Music (ASCAP).

Questions for Discussion

1. What did you think about the gospel before you were a believer?

2. Why did I say that the phrase "as many as were appointed to eternal life believed" (v. 48) is mentioned? Do you agree with my assessment?

3. Do you have any experiential proof that a person does not have to be very articulate to proclaim the gospel?

4. Have you ever seen somebody become infuriated with the gospel? What happened?

5. Should we expect our missionaries to report back that people are being converted? Why or why not?

1 Now at Iconium they entered together into the Jewish synagogue and spoke in such a way that a great number of both Jews and Greeks believed. 2 But the unbelieving Jews stirred up the Gentiles and poisoned their minds against the brothers. 3 So they remained for a long time, speaking boldly for the Lord, who bore witness to the word of his grace, granting signs and wonders to be done by their hands. 4 But the people of the city were divided; some sided with the Jews and some with the apostles. 5 When an attempt was made by both Gentiles and Jews, with their rulers, to mistreat them and to stone them, 6 they learned of it and fled to Lystra and Derbe, cities of Lycaonia, and to the surrounding country, 7 and there they continued to preach the gospel.

Acts 14:1-7

Chapter Seven

Tenacity

Starting location: **Iconium**

Cities on the journey: **Iconium, Lystra, Derbe**

You might read the story about Paul and Barnabas ministering in Iconium (Acts 14:1-7) and say, "This is getting redundant." It is true that these "apostles" (v. 4) carried on a similar ministry to what previously transpired in Pisidian Antioch about 90 miles to the northwest (13:14-52). We should appreciate and learn from the repetition since it emphasizes what was important to the missionaries, and to God.

But the stories of the gospel coming to Pisidian Antioch and Iconium are not *identical*. For example, unlike in Antioch, Luke says that in Iconium "the Lord . . . bore witness to the word of his grace, granting signs and wonders to be done by their hands" (14:3b). Careful interpretation will answer the question, "In telling the Iconium story, why did Luke include this detail?"

Tenacious Missionaries

Iconium, less populated than larger cities of that day, was on the edge of a plateau well-supplied with rain, making it a commercially fruitful city.[29] But would it be an *evangelistically* fruitful location? Ultimately, the Iconium story highlights *tenacious missionaries proclaiming a credible message.* Whatever the results would be, Paul and Barnabas continued the mission, and their tenacity is prominent in at least three ways.

Proclaiming

First, they kept proclaiming the gospel.

> Now at Iconium they entered together into the Jewish synagogue and spoke in such a way that a great number of both Jews and Greeks believed. (14:1)

The persecution just experienced in Antioch did not stop the missionaries; back to the synagogue they went. Luke records that they "spoke in such a way" (lit., "so spoke") that the result was many conversions (v. 1). There was more happening as they spoke than simply verbalizing truths. They *really* believed what they were saying, and you could see it on their faces and hear it in their tone. They did not merely talk; they persuaded and pleaded. I wonder if tears occasionally filled Paul's eyes as he talked about forgiveness. Perhaps Barnabas' voice got quieter as he became more intense. These men gave themselves fully to the preaching of the gospel because they knew that God convicts and saves when it is proclaimed.

JoAnne Shetler was a Bible translator among the Balangao people in the Philippines, completing the New Testament

---

[29] J.N. Birdsall, "Iconium," in *New Bible Dictionary*, eds. I. Howard Marshall, A.R. Millard, J.I. Packer, D.J. Wiseman, 3rd ed. (Downers Grove, IL: InterVarsity Press, 1997), 494.

in their language in the early 1980s. Even before the New Testament was completed, the gospel was proclaimed to the Balangaos, and some were converted. At their church meetings, finished portions of the translation were read and explained, "sometimes with surprising results," Shetler notes. In her autobiography, she illustrated this.

> One Sunday a woman attended the service for the first time. She enjoyed the singing, but as they read the Scriptures, she became increasingly agitated. Finally, teeth clenched, she got up and slipped out.
>
> Later, while we were eating she stomped into Tony and Tekla's house, walked up to within inches of Tony and, in a fashion untypical of Balangaos, she accused him to his face.
>
> "The nerve of you! You invite me to your meeting and what do you do? You tell that man up in front every sin I have committed, and he goes and announces it in public. And not only that, but he reads it from a book! I'll never come again."
>
> People were offended by the Scriptures often enough that the elders made it a practice to announce before reading from the Word, "You're going to think we know something about you and we're exposing it. But, honestly, nobody's told us anything. This Book just uncovers hidden things. It's just the nature of the Book."[30]

The truth hurts, and then it heals; the gospel is powerful. Paul and Barnabas were convinced of this, so they kept on preaching it, and the result was "a great number of both Jews and Greeks" (i.e., Gentiles in this largely Greek city) became followers of Jesus.

---

[30] *And the Word Came with Power*, 5th ed. (Wycliffe Bible Translators, Inc., 2006), 123.

Staying

The tenacity of Paul and Barnabas was demonstrated in another way: *they stayed in town when opposition arose.*

> But the unbelieving Jews stirred up the Gentiles and poisoned their minds against the brothers. (14:2)

Once again during their travels, a coalition of unbelieving Jews and Gentiles came together to persecute "the brothers," presumably not only Paul and Barnabas, but also the new believers in Iconium. How did the missionaries respond?

> So they remained for a long time, speaking boldly for the Lord . . . (v. 3a)

The connection between verses 2 and 3 is not immediately clear. How are we to understand the "So" of verse 3? It could be that the opposition was an indication that God was working in Iconium, "so" (or therefore) Paul and Barnabas were motivated to press on even in difficult circumstances. But it is possible that a new idea is being introduced, specifically that part of the work of missions involves staying in a location, even when the persecution escalates, in order to continue to proclaim the gospel *for the sake of those who have already believed*. The missionaries' example of courageous ministry against a wave of opposition would have demonstrated to the new believers in Iconium that Jesus is worth any sacrifice, and it would have provided frequent opportunities for the apostles to minister to the young church.

Notice something about Paul in this episode: he was not a robotic machine who flatly shared about Jesus, coldly organized people into churches, and then moved on and never thought about them again. He had such a love for new believers and churches he started that, even when he was not with them, he spoke of the "daily pressure" he felt regarding his "anxiety for all the churches" (2 Corinthians 11:28). So it was a loving concern for the immediately persecuted new Christians in Iconium that caused Paul and Barnabas to stay in that city "for a long time" (Acts 14:3a), perhaps the longest stop on the journey.

A Credible Message

Luke next adds the detail that as Paul and Barnabas "remained for a long time, speaking boldly for the Lord," the Lord "bore witness to the word of his grace, granting signs and wonders to be done by their hands" (v. 3). The "word of his grace" that these apostles proclaimed — the message of salvation by grace through faith in Christ — was confirmed by the Lord through the miracles they performed. These God-granted miracles were a way for the Lord to say, "What these men are saying is the truth!"

But there is something else to note, particularly regarding "signs and wonders." A contrast is seen between what the apostles were conveying versus what the unbelieving Jews were saying (v. 2).[31] A question this story presents is one of credibility: who should anyone believe, the unbelievers who were deceptive and embittered people against believers and the Lord, or Paul and Barnabas who were not only faithful and courageous as they spoke the words of life, but also demonstrably had God's support? Every unbeliever in Iconium should have seen which "side" had moral uprightness and the well-being of others as their goal. These tenacious missionaries proclaimed a *credible* message.

These miracles also would have been an ongoing encouragement to the believers in Iconium that the message

---

[31] I was pointed to this contrast by William J. Larkin, Jr., in his InterVarsity Press commentary on Acts, located at https://www.biblegateway.com/resources/ivp-nt/Final-Rejection-Plotters-Versus-Apostles, accessed September 3, 2021.

they had embraced was indeed true (cf. 5:12; 6:8; 15:12). And in thinking about the overall aim of the book of Acts, declarations like this about the accompanying miracles when the gospel was proclaimed to Jews and Gentiles should have strengthened the original readers of Acts (especially Gentile believers) in the faith. The same should be true for any believer today (cf. Hebrews 2:4).

Relocating

Miracles do not guarantee belief.

> But the people of the city were divided; some sided with the Jews and some with the apostles. (Acts 14:4)

Up to this point in the story, the persecution experienced by the believers in Iconium was at an "intellectual" level, but it was about to become physical, and perhaps deadly.

> When an attempt was made by both Gentiles and Jews, with their rulers, to mistreat them and to stone them . . . (v. 5)

This led to the third way Paul and Barnabas demonstrated tenacity as missionaries: *they went elsewhere to preach the gospel when the persecution was about to get severe.* Somehow they "learned of" persecution that was about to become violent, so they "fled to Lystra and Derbe, cities of Lycaonia, and to the surrounding country, and there they continued to preach the gospel" (vv. 6-7).

I hear you wondering, "They left town before the worst persecution came? That sounds like the opposite of tenacity!" But a missionary leaving an area and avoiding physical pain does not automatically make him a coward. His departure could be calculated for gospel advance, which it was for Paul and Barnabas as they traveled the twenty miles southwest from Iconium to Lystra and then about sixty more miles from Lystra to Derbe. Both of these towns were smaller, and we cannot know for sure if they originally intended to go to these locations, but once there, Kingdom-advancing ministry continued.

It might have been more masochistic than evangelistic for Paul and Barnabas to stay in Iconium. That Luke ends this episode (14:1-7) with "and there they continued to preach the gospel" puts a positive light on their decision. They remained tenacious; they persevered in proclaiming the credible message about the Lord's grace.

Stirred and Assured

How does this story speak to believers today?

First, it should stir us to remain tenacious for the Lord. I have in mind persevering in gospel proclamation, but also remaining committed to the Lord even when it brings opposition. Do not let familiarity with these stories numb you to the examples these men are. The Iconium account, though brief, is a case study in missiological practice. Missionaries today who want to honor the Lord with their time and ministries would all say, "I want to be known as a man who is tenacious for Jesus." In the Iconium story alone, the Lord has provided an exemplary model of persevering faithfulness. If you are a missionary, you might know much about William Carey, or Adoniram Judson, or John Patton. But beyond even these wonderful servants of the past, make sure you have thought through the entire ministry of Paul (not only Acts 14:1-7) with far more scrutiny and humility and eagerness to imitate *him*. After all, his story is in the Bible.

A thorough study of Paul's ministry would not only include the book of Acts, but also at least 1 Timothy, 2 Timothy, and Titus, because in those letters Paul wrote to his "representatives" who carried on his ministry while he was absent, showing us the heart of the missionary *par excellence*.[32] What might become of the missions enterprise globally if there was a recovery of a "Pauline" approach to missions?

Second, the Iconium story should assure us in a godless culture full of false messages that the gospel of Jesus is the one eternally reliable, saving message. It seems that in increasing measure regarding matters of righteousness, the trajectory of society is headed into more and more depravity. I sometimes find myself asking, "If it is this bad now, what is it going to be like for my children in a few decades? And what about their children?" The story of the gospel going to Iconium is a reminder that, like then, the gospel is the great need of our day, God's kingdom will advance, and in Christ alone is eternal life.

Like in Iconium, those against Christ will seek to keep the hearts of unbelievers in the dark by filling their minds with lies. Those who have come to the light will be tempted to shrink back into the darkness. But at the end of life, we each will have embraced one of two messages. Some will embrace a message and worldview that has no foundation, no ultimate answers, no record of saving a single soul, and no hope. All others will have believed a story of grace and forgiveness and reconciliation to God and freedom from sin's enslaving power. This second option promises a future day when we will be completely set free from sin's egregious presence and we will experience nothing but joy with resurrected, glorified bodies on a new earth forever and ever.

---

[32] For further consideration of the roles of Timothy and Titus under Paul, see Steve Burchett, "The Role of Timothy and Titus: Apostolic Representatives, Not Pastors," https://www.ccwtoday.org/2020/07/the-role-of-timothy-and-titus-apostolic-representatives-not-pastors/, accessed August 13, 2021.

Why would we ever choose anything or anyone but Jesus?

_____

We have now observed multiple times the gospel being proclaimed to Gentiles who had significant knowledge of the God of the Jews. But the audience is about to change. What will the missionaries say, then?

Questions for Discussion

1. To this point in the story, approximately how many miles does it appear the missionaries have traveled (both on the water and land) since they left home (Antioch in Syria)? You can calculate this by looking at the map prior to chapter 1. Is the mileage they have covered so far surprising to you?

2. What was the significance of the Lord "granting signs and wonders to be done" by the apostles? Should that be happening today?

3. In what ways does the Iconium story speak to life in a culture that is shifting into more depravity?

8 Now at Lystra there was a man sitting who could not use his feet. He was crippled from birth and had never walked. 9 He listened to Paul speaking. And Paul, looking intently at him and seeing that he had faith to be made well, 10 said in a loud voice, "Stand upright on your feet." And he sprang up and began walking. 11 And when the crowds saw what Paul had done, they lifted up their voices, saying in Lycaonian, "The gods have come down to us in the likeness of men!" 12 Barnabas they called Zeus, and Paul, Hermes, because he was the chief speaker. 13 And the priest of Zeus, whose temple was at the entrance to the city, brought oxen and garlands to the gates and wanted to offer sacrifice with the crowds. 14 But when the apostles Barnabas and Paul heard of it, they tore their garments and rushed out into the crowd, crying out, 15 "Men, why are you doing these things? We also are men, of like nature with you, and we bring you good news, that you should turn from these vain things to a living God, who made the heaven and the earth and the sea and all that is in them. 16 In past generations he allowed all the nations to walk in their own ways. 17 Yet he did not leave himself without witness, for he did good by giving you rains from heaven and fruitful seasons, satisfying your hearts with food and gladness." 18 Even with these words they scarcely restrained the people from offering sacrifice to them.

19 But Jews came from Antioch and Iconium, and having persuaded the crowds, they stoned Paul and dragged him out of the city, supposing that he was dead. 20 But when the disciples gathered about him, he rose up and entered the city, and on the next day he went on with Barnabas to Derbe.

Acts 14:8-20

Chapter Eight

Reach

Starting location: **Lystra**

Cities on the journey: **Lystra, Derbe**

National Public Radio (NPR) once misdefined Easter, calling it, "the day celebrating the idea that Jesus did not die and go to hell or purgatory or anywhere at all, but rather arose into heaven."[33] When online readers caught the mistake and informed NPR, they quickly corrected the post to say that Easter is "the day Christians celebrate Jesus' resurrection."

Examples abound of biblical illiteracy today. Yet the next stop on the first missionary journey, Lystra, was populated with people who were even more clueless about Scripture.

It would have taken Paul and Barnabas about a day to walk the twenty miles south from Iconium to Lystra, which was not located on the main road. There must have been few Jews

---

[33] Elizabeth Jensen, "NPR Catches Hell Over Easter Mistake," https://www.npr.org/sections/publiceditor/2018/04/02/598029102/npr-catches-hell-over-easter-mistake, accessed August 22, 2020.

in that city because there is no record that the missionaries went into a synagogue. Instead, Paul and Barnabas found themselves among highly superstitious pagans who, unlike those in a Sabbath day meeting in a synagogue, had no basic knowledge of God's redemptive program and promised Messiah. Yet we see in this story that *the gospel was even for superstitious, pagan Gentiles.*

This episode should help us think about ministry to people with little to no Bible background. But before considering that, we should observe the story itself.

Speaking and Healing in Lystra

The first significant event in Lystra, located on the elevated plains of Lycaonia, was *not* Paul healing a crippled man, but when this man "listened to Paul speaking," probably in the *agora*, the public marketplace. For three reasons, there should be no doubt that Paul was proclaiming the truth about the Lord. First, the word for "speaking" has just been previously used for proclaiming the gospel (cf. 13:42 [translated "told"], 45; 14:1). Second, in the immediately preceding verses (14:6-7), it distinctly says that after fleeing Iconium, Paul and Barnabas "fled to Lystra and Derbe" where "they continued to preach the gospel." Third, the healing of the crippled man must have happened in order to confirm the message being shared (cf. 14:3).

The man "who was crippled from birth and had never walked . . . had faith to be made well" (vv. 8b-9), likely because of what Paul was communicating. It is possible that this could be translated, "had faith *to be saved*," but "be made well" is preferred. If the man had the faith necessary "to be saved," he already would have been. The story only makes sense if it is about this man's belief regarding what Paul could do for him physically. So Paul, recognizing his faith, and using "a loud voice" so that everyone heard, commanded, "'Stand upright on your feet.' And he sprang up and began walking" (v. 10).

Pagan Worship

But then something unusual happened: the crowd began to worship Paul and Barnabas, saying, "The gods have come down to us in the likeness of men!" The missionaries probably did not initially understand their words because the worshippers spoke in Lycaonian (v. 11; cf. v. 6). They even had names for the missionaries: "Barnabas they called Zeus, and Paul, Hermes, because he was the chief speaker" (v. 12). Soon the worship became even more potentially serious and extravagant when the "priest of Zeus, whose temple was at the entrance to the city, brought oxen and garlands to the gates and wanted to offer sacrifice with the crowds" (v. 13).

Why were these citizens of Lystra acting like this and talking about these men in such dramatic categories? Eckhard J. Schnabel explains.

> There was a legend, attested in Phrygia, according to which two local gods — perhaps Tarchunt and Runt, or Pappas and Men (in the Greek version of the legend the gods Zeus and Hermes) — wandered through the region as human beings. Nobody provided them with hospitality, until Philemon and Baucis, an older couple, shared their supplies with the unrecognized gods. The couple was richly rewarded. They were told to climb a mountain, which they did, with the result that they escaped the flood which consumed the others (*Ovid Metamorphoses* 8 626-724).[34]

As Paul and Barnabas began to minister, the Lystrans apparently were thinking the gods were among them again.

---

[34] *Paul the Missionary*, 86.

They called Paul, the one speaking, "Hermes," the Greek god of oratory, and they called Barnabas "Zeus," the king of the gods, perhaps because he appeared to be in the background overseeing and ruling everything. These pagans did not want to make the same mistake that everybody but that elder couple did previously!

Rejecting Pagan Worship

Once the priest appeared with the oxen (the animals to be sacrificed) adorned with garlands, the missionaries knew exactly what was happening, and so they dramatically rejected their worship. They first "tore their garments" (v. 14), an expression of grief and possibly a physical gesture to call the crowd's behavior blasphemy. And then they demonstrated their angst by asking, "Men, why are you doing these things?" (v. 15a).

Paul saw this as an opportunity to tell these people about "a living God" (v. 15). The starting place of the message in Lystra was different than in Antioch and Iconium. In those cities, the missionaries went to Jewish synagogues where people understood the content of the Old Testament. However, most in Lystra were not only ignorant of redemptive history (known through the Old Testament), but they also were self-deceived regarding the doctrine of God. So in order to proclaim the truth about God, Paul started with a declaration about their humanity in response to the people calling them gods: "We also are men, of like nature with you . . . " (v. 15b). And he called for a change of direction, telling the Lystrans to "turn from these vain things to a living God." They were worshippers of worthless idols, but now were hearing about the awesome God who is alive, the creator of everything. Paul told them the "good news" that they could escape from such vanity and, it is implied, come to know and be reconciled to the one true God. We can assume Paul's aim was to reveal that this is only possible through the ministry of Jesus, but there is no indication he was able to.

Paul proceeded to explain God's past disposition, that "he allowed all the nations to walk in their own ways" (v. 16). Previously, there was no immediate judgment (which they deserved), but also no saving truth. However, God still revealed himself to them through his merciful activity, "giving rains from heaven and fruitful seasons" (v. 17a). Consequently, they all knew the human experience of having hearts satisfied "with food and gladness" (v. 17b).

How did the Lystrans respond to this God-centered preaching? "Even with these words they scarcely restrained the people from offering sacrifice to them" (v. 18). They were not understanding *at all*.

Severe Persecution

While the missionaries were ministering in Lystra, Jews from Antioch and Iconium once again plotted and attempted to thwart the gospel's advance (v. 19a). Like in previous locations, a coalition of Jews and Gentiles came together and rallied Lystrans to join them in opposing Paul by stoning him (the punishment for blasphemy; cf. Leviticus 24:14). Their bloodthirsty nature is even more pronounced when you consider that some of these Jews came from Iconium 20 miles away, but others came from Pisidian Antioch about 100 miles from Lystra!

They located Paul, and so did the stones, flying from the persecutors' hands. I imagine he first tried to run, but perhaps one struck the back of his skull and he collapsed, curling up in a ball on the ground, desperately trying to cover his head with his arms until, suddenly, he stopped flinching; he stopped crying out; he even stopped moaning. Assuming Paul was dead, they took his listless body out of the city to rot (v. 19b).

Back to Lystra, On to Derbe

But Paul was not dead. He got up and returned to Lystra, "and on the next day he went on with Barnabas to Derbe" (v. 20), about a three day trip if walking.

Who were "the disciples" who "gathered about him" (v. 20a) right before he arose and went back into Lystra? Does this refer to Barnabas and a few others on the apostle's team that we have not previously heard about?

Maybe we were not told the whole story of what happened in Lystra, especially before the pagans started worshipping Paul and Barnabas. Remember that Paul was "speaking" (v. 9) when he healed the crippled man. It is possible that in that more peaceful setting, perhaps with a few Jews in town listening, he spoke of Jesus' death and resurrection, and then some *did* come to Christ. After all, Timothy's Jewish grandmother Lois and mother Eunice (cf. 2 Timothy 1:5) were from Lystra (cf. Acts 16:1). Were they some of "the disciples" who surrounded Paul and walked with him back into Lystra after his gruesome beating? Did these new believers welcome him into their home and nurse him back to enough strength that he was able to depart the next day to preach in Derbe? And was Timothy there, watching it all (cf. 2 Timothy 3:11)? Likely so.

So What?

The message of grace was not only for Gentiles like Sergius Paulus who "sought to hear the word of God" (13:7), or Gentiles already within the synagogues, worshipping the God of the Jews. *The gospel was even for superstitious, pagan Gentiles.*

There is an interesting comparison to note between Paul's healing ministry and Peter's in Jerusalem (see Acts 3). First, each man they healed was "crippled from birth" (14:8 and 3:2, there translated "lame from birth"). Second, both Peter and Paul "looked intently" at the crippled men (14:9 and 3:4, there translated "directed his gaze"). Third, in both instances, the healed men leaped up and began to walk (14:10 and 3:7). This literary connection reveals the Lord's power and favor in both ministries and in both locations; the gospel is for Jews *and* Gentiles, even idol-worshipping pagans. Remember, it was the Lord who granted "signs and wonders to be done" by the hands of the apostles (14:3). Peter did this primarily among Jews in Jerusalem, and Paul performed these among not only the monotheistic Gentiles of the nations, but among polytheistic Gentiles who worshipped and feared multiple gods. The gospel was even for people like that!

And because it was God's purpose to save pagan Gentiles, the gospel was powerful in Lystra; lives were changed! The proof? I have already noted that some of "the disciples" who ministered to Paul after he was nearly stoned to death may have been new believers from Lystra. But if that was not the case, we know a church was born in Lystra because even though Paul departed from there the day after he was persecuted, he returned perhaps a few weeks or months later to minister to believers in Lystra and to appoint elders in the young church (cf. vv. 21-23). I am assuming that the new church included not only some of the few Jews in Lystra, but also pagan Gentiles.

Now What?

Think about some ways the Lystra story speaks to us about evangelism and missions, especially in settings where little Scripture is known and/or hearts are strikingly hard.

First, it teaches something strategic about presenting the gospel: we cannot assume people have even a basic understanding of the Bible, but they do know some truths about God, so we will often need to start there. I am not advocating proving God's existence, but following Paul's example by giving people proper categories and definitions for what they already know (God is creator) and have seen (God's activity in nature, and bringing forth provision for his creatures), and what they experience daily (satisfaction because of what God has provided).

Second, the Lystra story reveals the potential reach of the gospel: the good news about Jesus Christ is relevant for anyone, anywhere in the world, including those with the hardest hearts. Sometimes when the subject of missions is broached, there is a romantic idea in people's minds about "precious lost souls in the jungle" or "needy, helpless people in the slums." Those thoughts are not wrong, but are said with a bit of naivety about what is really going on around the world among lost people. For example, there are terribly disturbing, wicked practices happening like cannabalism, female genital mutilation, and polygamy. Yet no one is so bad that they could not be delivered by God's grace. That's true for a demon-possessed tribesman as well as your self-worshipping neighbor. The Lystra story charges us to move toward, not away from, people who seem impenetrable with the gospel. Jesus even died for people like that!

Third, the Lystra story points to God's role in the salvation of sinners: we must share the good news, but it takes a work of God in the heart of man if he is ever going to turn from his sin to Jesus. The hardness of the heart is on full display in verse 18: "Even with these words they scarcely restrained the people from offering sacrifice to them."

I am encouraged that even the great apostle Paul needed God's presence and power. If you have ever shared the gospel with someone and it was like your words clanked off of a concrete slab, I think you understand. However, by telling the pagans the good news, Paul did exactly what we all must do if we are going to see people converted to Christ. There *is* hope for that child who is now out of the house and has embraced homosexuality, and the alcoholic co-worker, and the unkind husband who has seemingly fallen out of love with you. They all might be radically changed by the gospel. It *is* possible. Tell them about Jesus, and rest in God's sovereignty.

What was the goal of Paul and Barnabas? Were they content to proclaim the gospel and then quickly move on? What about the new believers who would be left behind? The next two chapters will give us answers to those significant questions.

Questions for Discussion

1. What is the most interesting part of the Lystra episode to you? Why?

2. How might Paul's message in Lystra help us in our evangelism?

3. What romantic or wrong thoughts about missions have you ever had or heard?

4. Is God's role in the salvation of sinners encouraging to you? Talk about it.

20 . . . and on the next day he went on with Barnabas to Derbe. 21 When they had preached the gospel to that city and had made many disciples, they returned to Lystra and to Iconium and to Antioch, 22 strengthening the souls of the disciples, encouraging them to continue in the faith, and saying that through many tribulations we must enter the kingdom of God.

Acts 14:20b-22

Chapter Nine

Aim

Starting location: **Derbe**

Cities on the journey: **Derbe, Lystra, Iconium, Pisidian Antioch**

It should now be evident in our study through Acts 13-14 that Paul and Barnabas proclaimed the gospel with frequency and zeal. From Salamis to Paphos to Pisidian Antioch to Iconium to Lystra to Derbe (vv. 20-21a), they shared the good news and saw both Jews and Gentiles believe in Jesus. But in Acts 14:21-23 we learn that their ultimate aim was more than to hear people profess faith in Jesus and then quickly move on to new territory to get more "decisions."

You might be tempted to skip this chapter because it may seem like it is only for those serving as missionaries. However, by considering the ministry of missionaries to new converts, we will also see what is essential for all of us from the moment we repent and believe in Jesus.

Missionary Activity Once They Believe

What did Paul and Barnabas do when individuals in a particular location professed faith in Christ?

Baptize

First, they baptized the believers and gathered them into new churches.

Baptism? Where is that mentioned? It is not explicitly. However, in speaking about their ministry in Derbe, Luke writes, "When they had preached the gospel to that city and *had made many disciples . . .*" (v. 21, emphasis added). The only other uses in the New Testament of the Greek word for "made disciples" are found in Matthew 13:52; 27:57; and 28:19. It is that final verse that is especially significant for our understanding of what was happening not only in Derbe, but in each location on the journey once people turned to Christ.

At the end of Matthew 28, the resurrected Jesus commissioned his apostles.

> And Jesus came and said to them, "All authority in heaven and on earth has been given to me. Go therefore and make disciples of all nations, baptizing them in the name of the Father and of the Son and of the Holy Spirit, teaching them to observe all that I have commanded you. And behold, I am with you always, to the end of the age." (vv. 18-20) .

Part of making disciples included baptizing those who became followers of Jesus. This was the immediate practice of the apostles who then passed on the teaching of Jesus. As the years went by and the gospel went forth, the teaching of Jesus and the responsibility to baptize disciples was passed on. Therefore, we can only assume that what is meant by "made many disciples" in Derbe (Acts 14:21) is that some in that town believed in Jesus and were immediately baptized.

But once they believed and were baptized, then what? Since each of these stops were pioneer locations (no existing churches), the missionaries brought the believers together forming a local church — a community of baptized believers who gathered with each other regularly and followed Christ together. We know this is what happened because we read that the missionaries returned to Lystra, Iconium, and Antioch and "appointed elders for them *in every church*" (v. 23, emphasis added). In order for there to be elders who shepherd a church, there has to be a body of believers committed to one another who then submit themselves to the men appointed to lead them. Methodologically, then, Paul and Barnabas were not only concerned about hearing people profess faith in Christ and baptizing them, but baptism was a doorway into the fellowship of a local church.

For one year in college, I was part of a street evangelism ministry on Friday evenings in a large city. Our goal was to get people to "make a decision for Christ," and at the end of the night we reported our numbers to the rest of the team. I look back on those days and admire the zeal we all had to tell others about Jesus. But we were not careful to truly make disciples, which would have required ongoing teaching and encouragement regarding obedience to Jesus, and helping people to get into solid churches. Sure, we would give people a Bible, and encourage them to "go to church on Sunday," and maybe even arrange to meet with them the following Friday evening, but as far as we were concerned, "Once saved, always saved!" When we had a decision for Jesus, mostly what was left to do was to report our numbers.

I am not averse to talking about numbers when thinking of the progress of the gospel. We even see actual numbers of believers mentioned in Acts (see 2:41; 4:4). But "counting converts" is not the end goal of evangelism; the aim is to make disciples. But even that can sound too individualistic if we are not careful. The hope is not only to lead a person to Jesus, but once they are submitting to Jesus individually, they are to follow him in community with others in a local church, starting with a public profession of faith via baptism. That was the strategy of Paul and Barnabas, in obedience to Jesus, and it should be our strategy as well.

What else did Paul and Barnabas do once there were believers in a particular location?

Strengthen

Second, they spoke motivating and sobering words to strengthen the churches they started.

It will not always be the case that missionaries are driven out of a location through persecution, but that was what happened to Paul and Barnabas in Antioch, Iconium, and Lystra. What is noteworthy about the geography at this point of the journey is that once they arrived in Derbe, they could have traveled east on a well-paved Roman road through familiar territory for Paul that included his hometown of Tarsus in Cilicia. Less than 200 miles from Derbe in that direction was their return destination of Antioch in Syria. But instead of heading east to safety, they went northwest back to the locations where they were previously despised and lied about and even, in Paul's case, severely beaten.

Missionaries are courageous. There were men in Ethiopia known as "running preachers" during the Italian occupation of that country (the years leading up to and during the Second

World War). They were also called "night preachers" because they would only come out around midnight and go into villages and preach the gospel, baptize new believers, and establish them in the faith. Before dawn they would go back into hiding either at their home or in the surrounding forests. Missionary Dick McLellan, who ministered with two of the approximately twelve "running preachers," explains the danger these men were in regularly.

> The Italian soldiers hunted these brave evangelists and put a price on their heads. Some of them were caught and killed or severely punished and imprisoned. Some were betrayed for the reward. All suffered great hardship and only a few survived the war without permanent physical damage.[35]

Paul and Barnabas *had* to take the dangerous route home. Why? Because there were beloved new believers in Lystra, Iconium, and Pisidian Antioch who needed to be built up. "[S]trengthening the souls of the disciples" (v. 22a; cf. 15:41; 18:23) is a fundamental activity of a missionary, even if the risk is extreme.

Continuing in the Faith

We are told of two ways that Paul and Barnabas strengthened the believers in each location. First, they did this by "encouraging them to continue in the faith" (v. 22b).[36] The new believers were to persevere in sound doctrine that was centered on the ministry and teaching of Jesus Christ. The idea is similar to the charge in Antioch to "continue in the grace of God" (13:43), but here it means more than just, "Persevere in believing in salvation by grace through faith in Jesus Christ." It would have included that, but the apostles were exhorting the

---

[35] *Warriors of Ethiopia* (UK: Lost Coin Books, 2014), 142.
[36] "Strengthening" and "encouraging" are mentioned together in Acts 15:32 as the ministry done by the prophets Judas and Silas in the church in Syrian Antioch.

new disciples to remain committed to all of the truth that they had learned from these messengers of Jesus. They were to be like those new believers in Jerusalem who, immediately after they were converted, "devoted themselves to the apostles' teaching" (2:42). Even new believers can and must study and know their Bibles.

Expecting Suffering

The second way that the missionaries strengthened the believers in Lystra, Iconium, and Antioch was by telling them that "through many tribulations we must enter the kingdom of God" (14:22c). We already know that Paul and Barnabas had experienced persecution and suffering throughout their journey, and we can only assume that the new believers faced similar tribulations once the apostles were gone. Now that the missionaries were back among these churches, there was no thought such as, "If you have enough faith, you will not suffer." It was the opposite: "Following Christ will be costly!"

Paul and Barnabas would have previously taught these people about entering God's kingdom. The kingdom of God partially arrived when Jesus was on the earth. The consummated kingdom will come in the future when Jesus returns and his followers enjoy a new earth without suffering, an unimaginable eternity of nothing but joy and righteousness and peace and love. The believer experiences small tastes of that even while on this present earth, and then at death he gets an incredible foretaste of what is yet to come when he is instantly with Jesus. But followers of Jesus will enjoy the kingdom completely in resurrected, glorified bodies once Christ returns to fully establish it on earth. Before they left, Paul and Barnabas made sure that these new believers had the right perspective about what will happen *before* that glorious eternal state.

Following Jesus is never going to be easy. At a minimum, you will be ridiculed; you will be called narrow-minded and unloving. You could lose your job because of what you believe. It is possible you could lose your life. But on the day you see Jesus face-to-face, you will not regret one second of even the worst suffering you experienced. These are essential ideas that must be communicated to new believers.

John Bradford lived in Britain in the 16th century. He was born around 1510, converted in 1547, and he became a "roving chaplain" in 1550, rebuking sin and preaching Christ. Eventually, the rule in Britain was handed over to a rogue regime set against the gospel. The ensuing persecution was fierce, and Bradford was imprisoned because of his love for Christ. He was ultimately condemned to die by wicked men. Another believer, 19-year-old John Leaf, was to be killed beside Bradford. Finally, the day of their martyrdom arrived. Faith Cook tells what happened next.

> Approaching the stake, both men fell on their faces in one brief moment of silent prayer. "Arise and make an end," said the sheriff impatiently, "for the press of the people is great." And so the martyrs were chained to the stake. Just moments before the fires were lit, John Bradford lifted up his face and hands in one last plea to his countrymen: "O England, England, repent thee of thy sins. Beware of false anti-christs; take heed they do not deceive you." He asked forgiveness of any he might have wronged and freely forgave those who so grievously offended against him. After begging the prayers of the people, he turned to address young John Leaf, his fellow-sufferer. The words are unforgettable: "Be of good comfort brother; for we shall have a merry supper with the Lord this night!"[37]

---

[37] Faith Cook, *Singing in the Fire* (Carlisle, PA: Banner of Truth, 2008), 7-8.

First, suffering. Then, reward.

The ministry of Paul and Barnabas to new converts not only speaks to the efforts of missionaries today, but it is a valuable reminder of what we all need to experience and believe once we are followers of Jesus. In the next chapter, two more actions of the missionaries will be considered. Yet again, the information will be useful for all believers, not just missionaries and their workers.

Questions for Discussion

1. How significant is baptism in your church? Why?

2. I mentioned that from Derbe, the missionaries could have traveled east through familiar territory in order to return safely home. Instead, they went the opposite direction into territory where they were previously persecuted. Trace this on the map located prior to chapter 1. What do you think about their decision?

3. Read 14:22. What is "the kingdom of God?"

4. Does the truth that "through many tribulations we must enter the kingdom of God" (v. 22) create any emotions within you? Explain.

5. In what ways are your church's missionaries similar or dissimilar in their ministries to what we have seen in Paul and Barnabas?

23 And when they had appointed elders for them in every church, with prayer and fasting they committed them to the Lord in whom they had believed.

Acts 14:23

Chapter Ten

Aim (continued)

Starting location: **Lystra**

Cities on the journey: **Lystra, Iconium, Pisidian Antioch**

Two of my children were part of a local church's sports ministry that culminated in a season-ending gathering of hundreds of athletes and their families to hear a speaker. I knew what to expect because I was converted in the context of a sports ministry that included similar tactics that were employed that night, especially when a "special speaker" was in town.

What tactics?

Typically, the speaker either is famous (such as a professional athlete), or he has a special skill (such as spinning basketballs on both hands while walking on stilts). The speaker first talks about his life or demonstrates his unique talent. He then shares a few verses from the Bible and tells the listeners that they need to "accept Jesus into their hearts" (not a New Testament idea) in order to go to heaven. He concludes by asking anyone in the audience to "pray this prayer with me in order to be saved" (the so-called "sinner's prayer," which, also, is not found in Scripture).[38]

Do you ever wonder what Paul would think if he walked into one of these contemporary settings? I am sure he would rejoice wherever the gospel is proclaimed, but he certainly would shake his head (did they do that in the first century?) at the unbiblical approach to calling people to Christ. He also would be amazed at how little help is given to these new "believers." I hear him saying, "You are good at getting people to make decisions, but you are not making disciples!"

We have learned so far on the first missionary journey that when Paul and Barnabas led people to faith in Christ, they baptized and then gathered new believers into churches (14:21). And then, second, they further established these disciples with motivating words about persevering in sound doctrine and sobering words about the reality of suffering for Jesus Christ before the King returns (v. 22).

What else did the missionaries do once there were believers in a particular location?

Appoint Elders

They appointed elders in the churches they started.

In a local church, the terms "elders," "pastors," and "overseers" should be used to refer to the same group of men.[39] You will sometimes hear a church refer to its "pastor and elders," but technically they should all be referred to as both pastors and elders. We know from the rest of the New Testament that

---

[38] For a biblical analysis of these types of methods, see Jim Elliff, "Closing with Christ," https://www.ccwtoday.org/2020/02/closing-with-christ/, accessed August 17, 2021.
[39] See Acts 20:17, 28 where the terms "elders" and "overseers" are used to describe the same group of men who are charged "to care for [to pastor] the church of God" (v. 28; cf. Ephesians 4:11).

elders of a church must only be men (1 Timothy 2:11-15) who desire to serve in that capacity (3:1) and are qualified to fulfill such a role (3:2-7; Titus 1:6-9). Their ministry is primarily about teaching and equipping the church in a variety of settings (1 Timothy 5:17; Titus 1:9a; Ephesians 4:11-12), but they also are charged with protecting the flock from false teaching (Acts 20:28-31; Titus 1:9b) and praying with and for those in need (James 5:14).

None of these details are delineated in the story of the first missionary journey. We are simply told that once there were assemblies of disciples in a specific geographical location, Paul and Barnabas appointed multiple elders in each individual church (v. 23a). This does not mean that elders were put in place immediately after a church was formed. We can assume that Paul and Barnabas spent numerous hours over a number of days teaching and interacting with all of the believers, including explaining Christ's will for the leadership of a local church. Soon, some of the men who showed leadership potential received additional instruction and even opportunities to lead and share with the other believers in a teaching capacity. Eventually, through observation and interaction with all of the believers, and then prayerful discussion with potential leaders, Paul and Barnabas "appointed elders" in each church.[40]

So Quickly?

Two questions emerge from the historical setting in which this took place. First, how was Paul able to appoint elders so "quickly" in these cities? Remember that this journey actually

---

[40] There is some discussion that the Greek verb for "to appoint" can have the meaning "to elect by vote," and so possibly the elders in these churches were chosen by the congregation. However, the context and plain reading of the verse indicate that in this instance, it was the apostles who did the actual selection and appointment. This does not rule out the high probability that they did this through communication with the believers in a particular town. The overall expectation that a man be "above reproach" (cf. 1 Timothy 3:2; Titus 1:6) would have necessarily included making sure that was the case by talking with others in the church about the elder candidates.

spanned over approximately two years. We cannot know how long Paul and Barnabas were in each city, though we do know that they were in Iconium "for a long time" (Acts 14:3). Paul must have been in each location for enough time to thoroughly teach sound doctrine, and would have spent many hours a day with some men he thought might become elders.

It may also not be accurate to say that he was "quick" to appoint elders in these churches. From our perspective, and with unbiblical expectations like, "A man must have a degree from seminary before serving as a pastor in a church," we might have unwarranted timelines in our mind regarding when a man is ready. Paul did tell Timothy that a man who would serve as an overseer "must not be a recent convert" (1 Timothy 3:6a), but once again, is our definition of "recent" different than Paul's? Also, remember that he did not appoint elders in Antioch, Iconium, and Lystra until he returned.

Elders in Lystra?

Perhaps the harder question to answer is this: since Lystra was a city full of superstitious, pagan Gentiles (see chapter 8), how was it possible that some of those converted men were ready to serve as elders? If the men who were appointed in Lystra were converted from paganism, that truly displays the power of the gospel to change lives. Could that have happened? Yes. Did that happen? I am not so sure.

Another possibility is that there were Jews in that city (remember Timothy was from there, and his grandmother and mother were Jewish), but not enough for a synagogue (ten male heads of households). But among those few male Jews, some believed and, like in Antioch and Iconium, had a head start on foundational ideas such as the authority of Scripture (they knew the Old Testament well), the doctrines of God and creation, and God's plan for redemption through the promised

Christ. Perhaps in all of those cities, it was such men (along with Gentiles who worshipped in the synagogue) who, after faith in Christ, were trained and became the first elders.

Missiological Implications

Certain practical implications arise when thinking through this missionary practice of appointing elders. One is that a "church" can exist without elders. There is not a single illustration in the New Testament of a church beginning *with* elders already in place. This does not mean that a church cannot start with men who are recognized and function as elders, but unlike some church planting models I have observed through the years (such as one that had to have a salary in place for multiple pastors before they would ever "start" and call themselves a church), it is not required.

Yet we also see in this that a church should aim to have multiple elders. I have noticed on classified ads on websites of denominations that churches are often "looking for God's man to lead us." What they mean is that they are looking for a sole pastor. I believe the apostle Paul would ask those sincere people, "Why would you do that? You should be praying for multiple godly men to lead you."

Implications for Every Disciple

Think about what Paul's practice of appointing elders in each church means for any disciple of Jesus. In locations that have been reached with the gospel, especially larger cities, there are typically multiple decent churches. It is easy to float around from church to church and never finally land. But it is God's will for believers to be committed to a local church, and the biblical pattern for church leadership should result in every disciple of Jesus being cared for by a team of elders.

Some believers find themselves in a situation where there is only one pastor. Yet as men are trained and aspire to serve, if they meet the qualifications for elders, a shift from singular to plural leadership should take place.[41] All of Christ's people need a local church with multiple pastors who will teach them, equip them, admonish them, pray for them, protect them from fierce wolves, and sometimes even protect them from themselves.

As a pastor, I have had numerous conversations through the years with people thinking through God's will for their lives. They have in mind choosing college or getting married or career choices or where they should live. Sometimes, though, they are not even doing what is obviously the Lord's will by committing to a local church where they can know and serve and be strengthened by other believers and at the same time be under the careful watch of elders.

Pray and Fast

Fourth, what did Paul and Barnabas do once there were believers in a particular location? *They entrusted to the Lord the elders of the churches they started.*

> And when they had appointed elders for them in every church, with prayer and fasting they committed them to the Lord in whom they had believed. (v. 23)

The word "them" is used twice in verse 23. We might have a friendly debate about to whom the second "them" refers. Is it speaking of the elders, or the churches? The first "them" refers to the believers that made up the churches. Though I cannot be dogmatic, I believe the second "them" refers to

---

[41] To consider some practical benefits of a plurality of elders, see Steve Burchett, "The Head of the Church Knows Best: Benefits of Having a Team of Elders," https://www.ccwtoday.org/2019/10/the-head-of-the-church-knows-best-benefits-of-having-a-team-of-elders/, accessed November 8, 2021.

the elders of each church because the "prayer and fasting" that followed their appointment is similar to what happened for Paul and Barnabas just after they were "set apart" for the missionary journey (see 13:2-3). The discipline of "fasting" that accompanied these prayers demonstrates this was not a quick prayer upon departure, but a sustained final period of time in which the apostles did not eat a meal (or several) in order to devote that time to entrusting these men to the Lord.

We are reading about the affectionate hearts of these missionaries upon departure from these churches. This does not mean Paul's ministry with these believers was officially over. Galatians was probably written to these churches after his return to Antioch. We also have the record of two more visits to these churches in Acts 16:1-6 and 18:23. But in this moment on the journey, the missionaries knew that these elders would need God's strength if they would faithfully lead God's people. "Many tribulations" were ahead.

Earlier, I mentioned classified ads posted on websites of denominations. One other phrase that I often see, besides, "looking for God's man to lead us," is "part-time pastor." In reality, though, as I heard one man say, being a "part-time pastor" is like being a "part-time father," which is impossible! The responsibilities, the burdens, the weightiness, and sometimes the outrageous expectations or misunderstandings, are profound and can even become all-consuming. Therefore, pray for *your* elders. They need it more than you know.

With All Your Heart

I will end this chapter with an exhortation to missionaries. We have observed in chapters 9 and 10 the aim of missionary work. Give yourself *fully* to the type of extensive, loving ministry you see in Paul and Barnabas. Missionary work is not for distracted men.

In an article titled, "Netflix is Making it Harder to Be a Missionary," a leader for a ministry that seeks to reach lost youth in Tapei reflects on what he has observed regarding cross-cultural ministry.

> In recent years we've seen a trend of new missionaries who don't ever actually get out of the culture shock phase. Their laptops and smartphones provide them unlimited access to their families and own culture and it makes it much more difficult to do the work of incarnation . . . For missionaries of old, the day they said goodbye to their families to depart for the mission field might have been the worst day of their lives. But as soon as the boat pulled away, the wound started to heal . . . My fear for missionaries today is that even though they've left home physically, it is entirely possible to continue living there via social media and FaceTime. And that wound of leaving home is constantly being reopened.[42]

Beware of how even God's good gifts can sidetrack what would otherwise be a fruitful ministry. Wherever you are, be there with all of your heart for the joy of all those the Lord brings under your care.

It was now time for Paul and Barnabas to return to Antioch in Syria. But do not think these are only "trip details" that are insignificant compared to the entirety of Acts 13-14. These verses might help us to make sense of all that has come before. Keep reading!

---

[42] Rachel Kleppen, "Netflix Is Making It Harder to Be a Missionary," https://www.christianitytoday.com/ct/2019/september-web-only/missionary-netflix-streaming-internet-incarnation-technolog.html, accessed August 29, 2020.

Questions for Discussion

1. Read 14:23. Look at every word carefully. What does the phrase "appointed elders for them in every church" mean?

2. What are some of your thoughts about how elder appointment should happen today?

3. What are some benefits of having a team of elders instead of just one pastor?

4. What are some reasons it is important for you to be under the loving care of elders (pastors)?

5. What are some ways we can pray for pastors? Pause right now and pray for your pastor(s).

24 Then they passed through Pisidia and came to Pamphylia. 25 And when they had spoken the word in Perga, they went down to Attalia, 26 and from there they sailed to Antioch, where they had been commended to the grace of God for the work that they had fulfilled. 27 And when they arrived and gathered the church together, they declared all that God had done with them, and how he had opened a door of faith to the Gentiles. 28 And they remained no little time with the disciples.

Acts 14:24-28

Chapter Eleven

Participants

Starting location: **Pisidian Antioch**

Cities on the journey: **Perga, Attalia (seaport), Antioch in Syria**

In chapter 4, we learned about the Roman road system. Once Paul and Barnabas crossed the Mediterranean Sea from Cyprus and arrived in Pamphylia, they would have found the Via Sebaste and walked on a fairly smooth "expressway" to Pisidian Antioch. Yet Paul and Barnabas, on the first journey which covered approximately 900 miles on land (about 600 by sea),[43] did not always have the luxury of a Roman road. Historian Edwin M. Yamauchi explains, "Much of [Paul's] other travels in Galatia and Phrygia . . . were on unpacked tracks."[44]

This reminds us once again that we are reading about real people and events in Acts 13-14. Paul and Barnabas were actual men, sometimes enjoying the highly navigable roads built by the Romans, but other times traveling on the country

---

[43] Schnabel, *Paul the Missionary*, 122.
[44] "On the Road With Paul."

lanes, occasionally crossing flooded rivers, and possibly leaving imprints in the snow as they walked over the high passes in the mountains. And they preached the gospel to human beings who truly existed and who needed to be saved from their sins. Some of these people never stopped hating the missionaries and Jesus. Yet some came to Christ, and churches were born.

These stories are meant to remind believers about the power of the gospel, the worth of Jesus, and the heart of God for the lost all over the world. These two chapters should bolster our confidence in Christ, and also inspire us to participate fully in getting the gospel to the unreached all over the world. To help you see your role, we will consider who the key participants were in the first missionary journey. But before we get to that, we should observe how the journey ended.

Traveling Home, Reporting to the Church

Now that elders had been appointed in each church in Lystra, Iconium, and Antioch, "they passed through Pisidia and came to Pamphylia" (14:24). If the missionaries took the Via Sebaste when they first traveled from Perga to Pisidian Antioch (the western route; Acts 13:13-14), it is possible that they took the more difficult journey south through the Taurus Mountains because Luke says they "passed *through* Pisidia" (14:24, emphasis added).[45]

They eventually arrived at the coast to take a cargo ship home. Before reaching the port city of Attalia, they preached "the word in Perga" (v. 25). Soon they were back on the Mediterranean Sea, sailing toward Antioch (14:26). Once they ported in Seleucia and made it up to Antioch in Syria, they "gathered the church together" (v. 27).

---

[45] See Mark Wilson, https://www.sevenchurches.org/wp-content/uploads/2020/03/Route-of-Pauls-First-Journey-Wilson-NTS.pdf, accessed December 9, 2020.

What did these men look like upon arrival? I am guessing their outward appearance changed, especially Paul. Were some of his "marks of Jesus" he had on his body (Galatians 6:17) visible on his face? Both Paul and Barnabas might have been thinner than when the journey began. I see them both smiling widely, along with the believers who greeted them. They had been gone about two years, probably with little contact back home. What a reunion! And what stories these men had to share! And that is what they did, but they did not have to be quick. They were settling in for a lengthy stay (v. 28). Their next trip would be to Jerusalem to deal with theological controversy (Acts 15). For now, it was so good to be back with people they loved.

Participants Then

These final verses answer this question: Who took part in the first missionary journey, and what did they do?

Missionaries

Perhaps the most obvious answer would be Paul and Barnabas, "the apostles" (14:14) — the missionaries. A repeated word should be noticed in the text. In 13:2, the Holy Spirit said, "Set apart for me Barnabas and Saul for the *work* to which I have called them" (emphasis added). Now that the trip was over, they settled in "Antioch, where they had been commended to the grace of God for the *work* that they had fulfilled" (14:26, emphasis added).

What was their "work?" Fundamentally, it was proclaiming Jesus and gathering believers into local communities, teaching them sound doctrine with sobering, hopeful implications, and putting elders over them who would lead them as they followed Christ together. They had accomplished what the Holy Spirit sent them to do. As mentioned in the previous chapter, this does not mean they would never serve these churches again. But for now, they were able to report, "Mission accomplished."

The Church in Syrian Antioch

The opening and closing verses (13:1-3; 14:26-27) reveal that the believers in Antioch were also key participants in the first missionary journey. As mentioned in chapter 2, it is either the whole church, or the prophets and teachers of the church, who fasted and prayed for the missionaries before they left (13:3), commending them "to the grace of God" (14:26). I am sure the whole church prayed regularly for Paul and Barnabas while they were away. Once they returned, they "gathered the church together" (v. 27). All of the believers were eager to welcome them home and hear their report.

God

The most significant participant in the first missionary journey was not the missionaries, nor the church, but God himself. We have already highlighted the Holy Spirit's role in telling the church to "set apart for me" Barnabas and Saul (13:2), and he "sent them out" (v. 4a). This shows that the journey was not only instigated by the Holy Spirit, but that these men were designated to this role "for" the Holy Spirit; the whole mission was done by and for the Holy Spirit through his chosen instruments. One explicit illustration of this is given when Paul was "filled with the Holy Spirit" and was then able to speak sternly to Elymas the magician and declare that a temporary blindness would come upon him, which immediately did (vv. 8-11).

The language that Luke used to describe what was reported to the church in Antioch makes it even clearer that not only was God a participant in the first missionary journey, but his role was preeminent: "And when they arrived and gathered the church together, they declared *all that God had done with them"* (14:27, emphasis added). These men looked back on the journey and had to conclude that the only reason they accomplished anything of significance was because of God's grace. The Lord had been with them, protecting them and directing them and comforting them and propelling them on, day after day.

They also told the church about how God "opened a door of faith to the Gentiles" (v. 27). This not only prepares readers of Acts for the controversy that led to the Jerusalem Council in Acts 15, but the reality that God made this way in for Gentiles (cf. 1 Corinthians 16:9; 2 Corinthians 2:12; Colossians 4:3) is a major point of emphasis in these two chapters. The missionaries reported that God was targeting the *whole* Gentile world, and he was hitting the bullseye, saving all peoples. The only entrance requirement was faith in Jesus.

Participants Now?

In Acts 13-14, the gospel advanced by God's grace through Spirit-empowered, church-supported missionaries who preached the gospel to unbelievers often in the face of severe opposition, yet some believed the good news and were gathered into churches; God propelled his kingdom into the nations. This is a true story meant to encourage believers. But this is also an ongoing story. The same global need remains; there are still unbelievers throughout the world who need the gospel. How are they to be reached? With the same participants today as the first missionary journey: missionaries must go;[46] churches must support; God must accomplish it all through both instruments.

---

[46] In order to follow as closely as possible to the events of Acts 13-14, I will not include "missionary helpers" as a fourth category in this list, even though there is one brief mention of a helper (John Mark, 13:13). As I mentioned in chapter 2, missionary helpers fulfill a critical role in missions.

Missionaries

The plan to reach the nations still includes missionaries. As we reflect on all that Paul and Barnabas did, and the pain they endured, we are reminded once again of the quality of men churches should send (see chapter 2 for further development of this idea). Not only must they be sound doctrinally, zealous evangelistically, and able to establish churches, but they must be willing to do all of that in the context of persecution that could range from having their message contradicted to being physically accosted, even to death.

Churches

But not even the best-equipped man can thrive apart from the loving, prayerful support of people back home. Powerful preaching and fruitful ministry on the mission field *depend* on this. Paul understood this. Five times in his letters he asked for prayer. Here is one example: "Pray also for us, that God may open to us a door for the word, to declare the mystery of Christ, on account of which I am in prison — that I may make it clear, which is how I ought to speak" (Colossians 4:3-4).[47] God redeems sinners through the proclamation of the gospel by missionaries who are being prayed for back home.

James Fraser, a missionary to the Lisu people in China, wrote to his prayer partners, "I believe it will only be known on the Last Day how much has been accomplished in missionary work by the prayers of earnest believers at home."[48] You may never set foot in another country. Your morning may be busy getting the kids ready for school, or commuting into the city for work. You may be retired, or a recently converted teenager. Whatever your place in life, your prayers for missionaries matter exceedingly. And if you commit to pray for them, when

---

[47] See also Romans 15:30-32; Ephesians 6:19-20; 1 Thessalonians 5:25; 2 Thessalonians 3:1-2.
[48] Mrs. Howard Taylor, *Behind the Ranges: Fraser of Lisuland Southwest of China* (London: China Inland Mission, 1956), 47.

they return home you will be eager to welcome them with the rest of the church to "hear the latest" and to rejoice with them as they share.

God

Our prayers for missionaries are a reminder that the most significant participant in gospel advance is still God. We know missionaries need the power of the Spirit. We understand they need God's grace to minister in a different culture. We are aware that they will encounter "wicked and evil men" (2 Thessalonians 3:2) from whom they will need to be delivered. And, as wonderful as we think these men are, we know they have weaknesses and still fight sin personally. So we must look to God on their behalf and ask for his strength in their lives because he is the one who directs his people, he is the one who gives wisdom, he is the one who sanctifies, he is the one who protects, and he is the one who opens hearts and saves sinners.

There was a missionary in Central Asia who went to a village hoping to share the Christmas story with a group of Muslims. Instead, he says, "I had wandered into something God was doing long before I arrived. Here was an unreached people group, in the most remote mountains of the world, isolated until just the past few years, worshipping Jesus together." And he was told there were not a few believers there, but as many as 200!

This kind of gospel advance has been happening since Acts 13-14, and it is not going to stop until Jesus comes back to gather his people into his perfect kingdom. In light of this, I want to plead with you now in a similar way that Luke was pleading with his first century readers through the retelling of the first missionary journey: because this is all true, do not quit on Jesus!

The missionary from Central Asia continues:

> People like me shouldn't get to see this. How do I get to see the birth of a church in a new people group? What did I do to deserve that? How could I possibly be qualified to be part of this? I can just imagine the conversation around the throne of God:
>
>> 'Really, Lord? You want him there? Do you think that will work?' one of the angels asks.
>>
>> And God answers, 'Well, yeah, his language is frankly sub-par; he isn't exactly good at the work in general; but he is there. Besides, no one on earth is going to think he had anything to do with it, so it's kind of how I work.'

The missionary concluded, "Who could do something like this but our God?"[49]

I am guessing that when this missionary went home to report to his sending church, like Paul and Barnabas he shared all that God had done with him, through him, and, frankly, even regardless of him!

It has always been God's design to reach the nations, and he has chosen missionaries (and their helpers), and believers back home, to accomplish his goal. But every soul saved and each church planted is ultimately because "God gave the growth" (1 Corinthians 3:6). To the Lord alone be the glory in missions!

---

[49] "An Incredible Story of God's Saving Power," https://jdgreear.com/an-incredible-story-of-gods-saving-power/, accessed September 5, 2020.

Questions for Discussion

1. What have been your experiences welcoming missionaries home? How could your church improve in this area?

2. Recall all of the ways God is demonstrated as the primary participant in the first missionary journey. Why is this significant?

3. In what ways does the story about the missionary in Central Asia affect you?

4. What are some ways you could pray for your church's missionaries? Pause right now and pray for them.

Chapter Twelve

Now

My goal in this final chapter is to address various groups of people in the church with ways they can quickly, even right now, involve themselves in God's kingdom advance around the world. You might be tempted to skip to your designation, but I hope you will read them all.

To Missionaries

You have a gigantic role in something eternally significant. God is determined to save people "from every tribe and language and people and nation" (Revelation 5:9). He sent his Son to redeem these sinners, and Jesus gave his life on the cross for them! And now, just like Paul and Barnabas, you have the privilege to tell others about this crucified and risen King, and to organize new believers into churches. It sometimes seems impossible, and that is exactly as God designed it so that you will rely on him. Just like those early missionaries, you have the same Holy Spirit to empower your ministry. Never forget that.

Such a consequential role in God's redemptive program certainly warrants a careful study of what the Lord wants you to do. I am sure you have done significant research. However, in my travels I have often been surprised to meet missionaries who appear to have a very limited knowledge of what Scripture teaches regarding a very simple question: "What does a missionary do?"

Here is my suggestion: read Acts repetitively. I am not talking about just Acts 13-14, but the whole book. Acts has twenty-eight chapters, so on a "five days a week" reading plan, you could read three chapters a day. That gets you through Acts every two weeks. Imagine what you will learn if you do this for several months. After the first couple of times through, start taking notes. Perhaps you will want to begin with the initial question, "What does a missionary do?" Another reading might have you answer, "What was 'the gospel' that the apostles preached?" As you read, I would suggest asking these types of questions with others on your team, or perhaps other missionaries in the region. Meet a few times to discuss your findings. The insights will be profound.

Once you have repetitively read Acts (for three months? four?), move on to 1 Timothy, 2 Timothy, and Titus (thirteen chapters total). Repeat the same process with all of these books combined, or you could take just one of these smaller books and read it through four or five days a week for a month. Pray for insight. And always be ready to adjust and change as Jesus, the head of the church, speaks to you and directs you through his words. You really do not have time to do anything else.

To Missionary Helpers

We only have one illustration in Acts 13-14 of a "helper" or "worker" (John Mark), and he is not a good model in this portion of Scripture, even though later in the New Testament he was welcomed back on Paul's team (see 2 Timothy 4:11).

But as I mentioned in chapter 3, a study through Acts and Paul's letters indicates that Paul had close to forty "helpers" in various locations (including some women). Just because you are not technically a missionary, your role in the missions enterprise is vital.

I wonder, though, if you have ever studied Acts, plus Paul's letters to Timothy and Titus, with this question in mind: "What do missionary workers do?" I will make a similar suggestion to you that I made to missionaries: begin now reading Acts repetitively, and then move on to 1 Timothy, 2 Timothy, and Titus (see my thoughts in the previous section for a reading strategy, including the joy of reading and discussing with others). Here is an important distinction to remember as you begin your study: both men and women can serve in this "helping" role, although only men (such as Titus and Timothy) can fulfill certain ministry responsibilities (teaching, exercising authority in other ways) on behalf of the missionary.

To Believers Back Home

Missionary and missionary helper life can be grueling. One Bible translator in Cameroon, reflecting on her first term serving as a Bible translator with her husband, wrote this.

> We have developed a more realistic view of missions. The Lord may have used John Piper's passionate sermons to get us to the field, but we have found that any missionary zeal is often sapped by one round of malaria. We have learned that missions is a daily putting of one foot in front of the other. Missions is years of doing things that do not necessarily feel spiritual (like memorizing all the words for their different kinds of ants . . .), praying that, one day, the name of Christ will be exalted here. We are convinced that missions is 98% raw endurance and 2% zeal.[50]

---

[50] Stacey Hare, "Then and Now: How Our Perspectives Have Changed Throughout Our First Term," http://haretranslation.com/2017/02/20/then-and-now-how-our-perspectives-have-changed-throughout-our-first-term/, accessed February 10, 2021.

Those serving as missionaries or missionary helpers do not need only financial support (not talked about directly in Acts 13-14), and prayer support (see chapter 11), but I especially want to encourage you to consider giving them "relational support." Here is an example: an email sent by you to the missionary or helper just to check up on them and to say you are praying for them and "read every word" of their latest update will fill them with joy. It might just be the means God uses to spur them on that season, that month, that week, and most definitely that day!

Another idea to consider if they have access to the internet is to gather a few other believers from your church and connect with them online. Chat about both serious and not-so-serious matters. Pray with them. Express your love for them.

Sure, they need some of your money to keep going, and they definitely need your prayers, but they also need *you*. Some of you might even have the finances to visit them at "ground zero." Perhaps that is something you should do right away.

To Pastors

There is more to an elder's ministry than encouraging and supporting missions. I would not want to come off as saying, "If you are not talking about missions every week, then you are not being faithful." Nevertheless, our role in the promotion of missions is vital and varied. We *at least* must teach, train, pray, organize, and "release" (see chapter 2). Two or three of those activities should be happening right away if they are not already.

Once you have people ready to "go," then what? My attendance at a Christian college, seminary, and various conferences through the years has led to hearing more "consider missions" messages than I can count. What has often been a theme is,

"All or nothing!" In other words, it is as if the commitment to "go" must always be, "Once you get on that airplane, don't even think about looking back." I appreciate the sentiment, and could even find some Scripture that would support that *if it is undeniably clear that the person is supposed to serve in that capacity.*

However, perhaps we are too often skipping a critical step of evaluation. In many scenarios, there is wisdom in first sending the person to the field for a short time (three weeks? three months?). When they return, he or she can assess the experience with church leaders and members. After prayerful consideration both with the person, but also the trusted missionary and team who worked in partnership with you, the individual might be sent back for another experience (perhaps a tad longer, but maybe even much longer).

Nothing is lost in this strategy, and so much could be gained, even providing a way out if, for example, the situation on the mission field was not quite what was expected. A measured approach like this also demonstrates more pastoral care, and promotes an increased understanding of the individual's readiness and gifts. Not everyone is to be a missionary, but many can serve effectively in a "helper" role. It is usually best for a man to first serve as a helper for a season before becoming a missionary.

To All Believers

Henry Martyn was born in in 1781 and eventually went to study law at St. John's College in Cambridge, England. While there, he was converted to Christ and began attending Trinity Church where Charles Simeon was the pastor. Martyn eventually became Simeon's assistant. Simeon stirred Martyn's heart for missions by telling stories about William Carey's work in India, and at the same time, Martyn was eagerly reading the journals of David Brainerd, a missionary to Native Americans.

It soon became obvious that Henry Martyn was to be sent out of Trinity Church as a missionary, which happened in July of 1805.

> The two friends each showed, in a different way, a noble faith and loyalty towards their Lord — Martyn, in choosing what was then a far distant exile as the next step after his brilliant successes, Simeon, in speeding the departure of a man so gifted for influence in Cambridge, and to himself so dear.[51]

Martyn arrived in Calcutta in May of 1806. Six years later, at the age of 31, he died of tuberculosis and fever.

As Henry Martyn was dying, a portrait of him arrived in Cambridge for Charles Simeon. The following words of Simeon about the arrival and unveiling of the portrait demonstrate that he was overcome with emotion.

> I could not bear to look upon it, but turned away, covering my face, and, in spite of every effort to the contrary, crying aloud with anguish . . . Shall I attempt to describe to you the veneration and the love with which I look at it? . . . In seeing how much he is worn, I am constrained to call to my relief the thought in Whose service he has worn himself so much; and this reconciles me to the idea of weakness, of sickness, or even, if God were so to appoint, of death itself. I behold in it all the love of my beloved brother.[52]

Simeon's biographer, H.C.G. Moule, explains where the portrait was placed in Simeon's house, and his ongoing connection to it.

---

[51] H.C.G. Moule, *Charles Simeon* (London: Methuen and Co., 1892), 132-3.
[52] Ibid., 139-40.

The portrait was hung in Simeon's dining-room, over the fire-place. He used often to look at it in his friends' presence, and to say as he did so, with a peculiar loving emphasis, "There, see that blessed man! What an expression of countenance! No one looks at me as he does; he never takes his eyes off me and seems always to be saying, 'Be serious — be in earnest — don't trifle — don't trifle.' Then, smiling at the picture and gently bowing, he would add, 'And I won't trifle — I won't trifle.'"[53]

The stories of Paul and Barnabas, and other gospel-proclaiming, courageous missionaries since, such as Henry Martyn, are like a portrait hovering next to us daily saying, "Don't trifle! Don't trifle!" May that be the norm for us individually as we follow Christ, and may that always be the case in our churches as we involve ourselves seriously and earnestly in worldwide missions.

---

[53] Ibid., 140.

Questions for Discussion

Before discussing these questions, read Acts 13-14 once more.

1. Did you have a favorite stop on the first missionary journey? Why was it your favorite?

2. Has a study of the first missionary journey increased your confidence in Jesus? Talk about it.

4. In what ways has your view of missions been affirmed or adjusted through this study?

5. How might your church need to change in order to align itself with a more biblical pattern of missions?

6. In what ways are you going to participate more fully in missions as a result of this study through Acts 13-14?

Acts 13-14: Full Text

Starting City: *Antioch in Syria*

13:1 Now there were in the church at Antioch prophets and teachers, Barnabas, Simeon who was called Niger, Lucius of Cyrene, Manaen a lifelong friend of Herod the tetrarch, and Saul. **2** While they were worshiping the Lord and fasting, the Holy Spirit said, "Set apart for me Barnabas and Saul for the work to which I have called them." **3** Then after fasting and praying they laid their hands on them and sent them off.

Cities on the Journey: *Seleucia (seaport), Salamis and Paphos (on the island of Cyprus*)

4 So, being sent out by the Holy Spirit, they went down to Seleucia, and from there they sailed to Cyprus. **5** When they arrived at Salamis, they proclaimed the word of God in the synagogues of the Jews. And they had John to assist them. **6** When they had gone through the whole island as far as Paphos, they came upon a certain magician, a Jewish false prophet named Bar-Jesus. **7** He was with the proconsul, Sergius Paulus, a man of intelligence, who summoned Barnabas and Saul and sought to hear the word of God. **8** But Elymas the magician (for that is the meaning of his name) opposed them, seeking to turn the proconsul away from the faith. **9** But Saul, who was also called Paul, filled with the Holy Spirit, looked intently at him **10** and said, "You son of the devil, you enemy of all righteousness, full of all deceit and villainy, will you not stop making crooked the straight paths of the Lord? **11** And now, behold, the hand of the Lord is upon you, and you will be blind and unable to see the sun for a time." Immediately mist and darkness fell upon him, and he went about seeking people to lead him by the hand. **12** Then the proconsul believed, when he saw what had occurred, for he was astonished at the teaching of the Lord.

Cities on the Journey: *Perga, Pisidian Antioch, Iconium*

13 Now Paul and his companions set sail from Paphos and came to Perga in Pamphylia. And John left them and returned to Jerusalem, **14** but they went on from Perga and came to Antioch in Pisidia. And on the Sabbath day they went into the synagogue and sat down. **15** After the reading from the Law and the Prophets, the rulers of the synagogue sent a message to them, saying, "Brothers, if you have any word of encouragement for the people, say it." **16** So Paul stood up, and motioning with his hand said:

"Men of Israel and you who fear God, listen. **17** The God of this people Israel chose our fathers and made the people great during their stay in the land of Egypt, and with uplifted arm he led them out of it. **18** And for about forty years he put up with them in the wilderness. **19** And after destroying seven nations in the land of Canaan, he gave them their land as an inheritance. **20** All this took about 450 years. And after that he gave them judges until Samuel the prophet. **21** Then they asked for a king, and God gave them Saul the son of Kish, a man of the tribe of Benjamin, for forty years. **22** And when he had removed him, he raised up David to be their king, of whom he testified and said, 'I have found in David the son of Jesse a man after my heart, who will do all my will.' **23** Of this man's offspring God has brought to Israel a Savior, Jesus, as he promised. **24** Before his coming, John had proclaimed a baptism of repentance to all the people of Israel. **25** And as John was finishing his course, he said, 'What do you suppose that I am? I am not he. No, but behold, after me one is coming, the sandals of whose feet I am not worthy to untie.'

26 "Brothers, sons of the family of Abraham, and those among you who fear God, to us has been sent the message of this salvation. **27** For those who live in Jerusalem and their rulers, because they did not recognize him nor understand the utterances of the prophets, which are read every Sabbath, fulfilled them by condemning him. **28** And though they found in him no guilt worthy of death, they asked Pilate to have him executed. **29** And when they had carried out all that was written of him, they took him down from the tree and laid him in a tomb. **30** But God raised him from the dead, **31** and for many days he appeared to those who had come up with him from Galilee to Jerusalem, who are now his witnesses to the people. **32** And we bring you the good news that what God promised to the fathers, **33** this he has fulfilled to us their children by raising Jesus, as also it is written in the second Psalm,

"'You are my Son,
today I have begotten you.'

34 And as for the fact that he raised him from the dead, no more to return to corruption, he has spoken in this way,

"'I will give you the holy and sure blessings of David.'

35 Therefore he says also in another psalm,

"'You will not let your Holy One see corruption.'

36 For David, after he had served the purpose of God in his own generation, fell asleep and was laid with his fathers and saw corruption, **37** but he whom God raised up did not see corruption.

38 Let it be known to you therefore, brothers, that through this man forgiveness of sins is proclaimed to you, **39** and by him everyone who believes is freed from everything from which you could not be freed by the law of Moses. **40** Beware, therefore, lest what is said in the Prophets should come about:

41 "'Look, you scoffers,
be astounded and perish;
for I am doing a work in your days,
a work that you will not believe, even if one tells it to you.'"

42 As they went out, the people begged that these things might be told them the next Sabbath. **43** And after the meeting of the synagogue broke up, many Jews and devout converts to Judaism followed Paul and Barnabas, who, as they spoke with them, urged them to continue in the grace of God.

44 The next Sabbath almost the whole city gathered to hear the word of the Lord. **45** But when the Jews saw the crowds, they were filled with jealousy and began to contradict what was spoken by Paul, reviling him. **46** And Paul and Barnabas spoke out boldly, saying, "It was necessary that the word of God be spoken first to you. Since you thrust it aside and judge yourselves unworthy of eternal life, behold, we are turning to the Gentiles. **47** For so the Lord has commanded us, saying,

"'I have made you a light for the Gentiles,
that you may bring salvation to the ends of the earth.'"

48 And when the Gentiles heard this, they began rejoicing and glorifying the word of the Lord, and as many as were appointed to eternal life believed. **49** And the word of the Lord was spreading throughout the whole region. **50** But the Jews incited the devout women of high standing and the leading men of the city, stirred up persecution against Paul and Barnabas, and drove them out of their district. **51** But they shook off the dust from their feet against them and went to Iconium. **52** And the disciples were filled with joy and with the Holy Spirit.

Cities on the Journey: *Iconium, Lystra, Derbe*

14:1 Now at Iconium they entered together into the Jewish synagogue and spoke in such a way that a great number of both Jews and Greeks believed. **2** But the unbelieving Jews stirred up the Gentiles and poisoned their minds against the brothers. **3** So they remained for a long time, speaking boldly for the Lord, who bore witness to the word of his grace, granting signs and wonders to be done by their hands. **4** But the people of the city were divided; some sided with the Jews and some with the apostles. **5** When an attempt was made by both Gentiles and Jews, with their rulers, to mistreat them and to stone them, **6** they learned of it and fled to Lystra and Derbe, cities of Lycaonia, and to the surrounding country, **7** and there they continued to preach the gospel.

Cities on the Journey: *Lystra*

8 Now at Lystra there was a man sitting who could not use his feet. He was crippled from birth and had never walked. **9** He listened to Paul speaking. And Paul, looking intently at him and seeing that he had faith to be made well, **10** said in a loud voice, "Stand upright on your feet." And he sprang up and began walking. **11** And when the crowds saw what Paul had done, they lifted up their voices, saying in Lycaonian, "The gods have come down to us in the likeness of men!" **12** Barnabas they called Zeus, and Paul, Hermes, because he was the chief speaker. **13** And the priest of Zeus, whose temple was at the entrance to the city, brought oxen and garlands to the gates and wanted to offer sacrifice with the crowds. **14** But when the apostles Barnabas and Paul heard of it, they tore their garments and rushed out into the crowd, crying out, **15** "Men, why are you doing these things? We also are men, of like nature with you, and we bring you good news, that you should turn from these vain things to a living God, who made the heaven and the earth and the sea and all that is in them. **16** In past generations he allowed all the nations to walk in their own ways. **17** Yet he did not leave himself without witness, for he did good by giving you rains from heaven and fruitful seasons, satisfying your hearts with food and gladness." **18** Even with these words they scarcely restrained the people from offering sacrifice to them.

Cities on the Journey: *Lystra, Derbe, Lystra (again), Iconium, Pisidian Antioch*

19 But Jews came from Antioch and Iconium, and having persuaded the crowds, they stoned Paul and dragged him out of the city, supposing that he was dead. **20** But when the disciples gathered about him, he rose up and entered the city, and on the next day he went on with Barnabas to Derbe. **21** When they had preached the gospel to that city and had made many disciples, they returned to Lystra and to Iconium and to Antioch, **22** strengthening the souls of the disciples, encouraging them to continue in the faith, and saying that through many tribulations we must enter the kingdom of God. **23** And when they had appointed elders for them in every church, with prayer and fasting they committed them to the Lord in whom they had believed.

Cities on the Journey: *Perga, Attalia (seaport), Antioch in Syria (starting location)*

24 Then they passed through Pisidia and came to Pamphylia. **25** And when they had spoken the word in Perga, they went down to Attalia, **26** and from there they sailed to Antioch, where they had been commended to the grace of God for the work that they had fulfilled. **27** And when they arrived and gathered the church together, they declared all that God had done with them, and how he had opened a door of faith to the Gentiles. **28** And they remained no little time with the disciples.